ASSESSMENT IN TRANSITION:

MONITORING THE NATION'S EDUCATIONAL PROGRESS

The contents of this book were developed
under a grant from the Department of Education.
However, those contents do not
necessarily represent the policy of the
Department of Education and you
should not assume endorsement by the Federal Government.

Cover and interior design by Lorna J. Bennie
Typography and printing by Armadillo Press, Mountain View, CA

ASSESSMENT IN TRANSITION:

MONITORING THE NATION'S EDUCATIONAL PROGRESS

Panel Chairmen
Robert Glaser, University of Pittsburgh
Robert Linn, University of Colorado

Project Director
George Bohrnstedt, American Institutes for Research

THE NATIONAL ACADEMY OF EDUCATION

THE NATIONAL ACADEMY OF EDUCATION is composed of scholars and education leaders who "promote scholarly inquiry and discussion concerning the ends and means of education, in all its forms, in the United States and abroad." Our current active membership is limited to 125 scholars. The heart of the Academy is found in the lively discussions that take place in our regular meetings and in the special panels and committees that we establish. Throughout our 32-year history, the Academy has been called upon by governmental and other agencies to conduct special studies and reviews on education issues of public interest, ranging from desegregation to the teaching of reading to standards-based reform. During the past six years, a panel of the Academy has been monitoring, studying, and making recommendations concerning the conduct of the Trial State Assessments given since 1990 in conjunction with the National Assessment of Educational Progress. For the first time in the history of NAEP, these assessments allow state-by-state comparisons of education achievement; they have proven to be of great interest to educators. The Academy's Panel has prepared three in-depth biennial reports on the trial state assessments of 1990, 1992, and 1994. They also issued, at the request of the National Center for Education Statistics, which oversees the Panel's work, a special report on the setting of achievement levels in connection with NAEP.

To carry out the Panel's challenging assignment, the Academy engaged two outstanding education researchers, Robert Glaser and Robert Linn, as co-chairs, and George Bohrnstedt and his colleagues at the American Institutes of Research as subcontractors to assist in the conduct of the research and writing, as well as a panel of distinguished educators and researchers with diverse forms of expertise on the NAEP program. They have constructed and overseen an ongoing set of research and policy papers examining major issues concerning the state trials of NAEP, including validity, sampling, content, data analysis, and reporting issues. The Panel now concludes its work with a capstone report that reflects on broad, long-term issues regarding the future of state NAEP and its relationship to national NAEP.

Carl F. Kaestle
President, The National Academy of Education

TABLE OF CONTENTS

January 29, 1997

Pascal D. Forgione
Commissioner of Education Statistics
National Center for Education Statistics
Office of Educational Research and Improvement
555 New Jersey Avenue NW
Washington, DC 20208

Dear Pat:

On behalf of The National Academy of Education, I am pleased to transmit to you the final report of the Academy's Panel on the Evaluation of the NAEP Trial State Assessment, entitled *Assessment in Transition: Monitoring the Nation's Educational Progress*. In it, the Panel takes a step back from their previous detailed work and considers philosophical, technical, and policy issues concerning the National Assessment of Educational Progress, both in the near term and the long term.

This report has been reviewed and approved by The National Academy of Education's Executive Council, acting as a Committee of Readers. We are confident that it will help clarify issues and spur discussions about the role of NAEP in the 21st century.

I have visited the Panel's working meetings several times over the past four years, and I have always been very impressed with the level of commitment and expertise of its members, the complexity and importance of the issues, and the usefulness and wisdom of its reports. I would like to take this occasion, on behalf of The National Academy of Education, to thank its two distinguished co-chairs, Robert Glaser and Robert Linn, who have devoted countless hours and prodigious brain power to the task, as have the members of the Panel and its superb project director, George Bohrnstedt of the American Institutes for

Research. The Academy also thanks staff members from AIR, some of whom have been with this project throughout its six-year duration, as well as Debbie Leong-Childs, executive director of the Academy, for her expert administrative role. Finally, I would like to thank your predecessors in the Commissioner of Statistics office, Emerson Elliot and Jeanne Griffith, for their support and colleagueship, as well as Sharif Shakrani and other NCES staff members who have been involved in monitoring the project and joining in the long and important dialogue about NAEP. This capstone report is the culminating document of the Panel's evaluation effort. I trust it will be of assistance to NCES and the National Assessment Governing Board as they shape both the policies and the content of NAEP, striving to maintain NAEP as the "nation's report card," while accommodating new assessment techniques, changing education ideas, and changing practices in the nation's classrooms.

Sincerely,

Carl F. Kaestle
President, The National Academy of Education

EXECUTIVE SUMMARY

THE NATIONAL ASSESSMENT OF EDUCATIONAL PROGRESS (NAEP) is the nation's leading indicator of what American students know and can do. The high, technical quality of the assessment and its independence from unwarranted influences and political pressures have enabled NAEP to monitor trends in education achievement reliably since its inception in 1969. Moreover, as the only assessment administered to a large and representative sample of American students, NAEP has accurately tracked changes for educationally important subgroups of students, as well as for the student population as a whole.

Furthermore, in less than 10 years, NAEP has expanded the number of assessed students approximately four-fold; has undergone substantial changes in content, design, and administration; and has drawn to itself veritable legions of stakeholders and observers. Taken singly, each of these changes represents a notable advancement for NAEP. Taken together, however, they have produced conflicting demands, strained resources, and technical complexities that potentially threaten the long-term viability of the entire program. Some of the most significant developments contributing to the current strain on NAEP include:

- Expansion of the assessment to include state-by-state NAEP;

- Inclusion of more challenging performance tasks;

- Testing broader and more representative samples of students, including students with disabilities or limited English proficiency;

- Pressure to make NAEP standards based, in the absence of nationally agreed upon content and performance standards;

- Desire for international comparisons; and the

- Desire to link NAEP with state assessments.

As we approach the year 2000, the current press for education reform seems likely to continue. The central role of assessment results will also likely grow as we seek to understand the impact of these reforms on the achievement of the nation's children. Within this context, the potential role of NAEP and the challenges NAEP faces are enormous. As a result, NAEP is at a point where critical choices must be made about its future.

THE PURPOSE OF THIS REPORT

Several efforts are under way or have been completed that review the design, administration, and structure of NAEP as the National Center for Education Statistics prepares for the reauthorization of NAEP in 1998. Rather than being one more report that examines the redesign of NAEP in the short-term, *Assessment in Transition* is designed to provide a more fundamental examination of NAEP's role and purposes.

Specifically, the report suggests ways in which NAEP should broaden its conceptualization, assessment, and reporting of student achievement to achieve a new vision by the year 2015. The report draws on the six years of investigation and four previous reports of the National Academy of Education's Panel on the Evaluation of the NAEP Trial State Assessment (TSA).

Our vision for NAEP in 2015 is framed within the context of two fundamental challenges facing education today:

- We must redefine education achievement in terms of what students will need to know and be able to do to be productive and knowledgeable citizens in the 21st century, and

- We must create the education conditions that will support this vision of achievement for all Americans.

To achieve this vision, the following questions are addressed in this report:

- What is the role of NAEP in addressing the challenges facing education today;

- How will NAEP need to be changed in order to contribute to development of an educated citizenry prepared for the 21st century; and

- What research and planning are required to support these changes and thereby fulfill our vision for NAEP.

NAEP's Role in the Coming Decades

We believe that *the fundamental purpose of NAEP should be to inform the public and policy-makers about student achievement trends in the nation and the states. It should do so in a manner that stimulates democratic discussion and debate, and leads to informed decision-making for American education.* This purpose is consistent with the principles established for NAEP at its outset—producing reliable and valid information and using that information to track trends in education achievement. NAEP—with its frequent broad surveys of core subject areas, large and representative student samples, and sophisticated statistical techniques—has been well suited to this purpose. However, to meet the needs for the next century, NAEP's role must expand in several ways:

THE NEED FOR INNOVATION

1. *Expanding the definition of achievement:* Of prime importance is our recommendation that NAEP adopt a substantially broader definition of achievement than is being used currently, indicating that definition to the nation and why the change is being made. In particular, NAEP must signal to schools, parents, and policy-makers that current definitions of achievement will not be sufficient to meet the demands of 21st century society. One way to do this is to provide richer information and examples about the competencies of the nation's children and adolescents. Therefore, wherever the results support doing so, we recommend that NAEP content be reported using profiles of achievement (with separate subscores for knowledge and skills, problem solving and interpretation, and performance in groups), assuming that these profile scores can be shown to be valid and reliable. In addition, NAEP should continue to report overall scores and content subscales where appropriate. Finally, trends should be established to track improvement on each of these measures.

2. *Informing the nation:* NAEP should stimulate ongoing dialogue and debate about changes needed in American education by presenting the results in ways that capture the attention of parents, superintendents, teachers, and policymakers at the national, state, and local levels. Shortly after the release of NAEP results, a series of informational events should be orchestrated. Specifically, we recommend that the Secretary of Education and Commissioner of Education Statistics encourage the major television networks, leading national newspapers, and other publications to do extended feature stories on what the nation's children know and don't know, within the context of what they need to know. We also recommend that the Department make broadly available stimulating materials, including videotapes of actual student performance, that can be used to encourage discussions at the state and local level.

3. *Setting valid standards:* Given the growing importance and popularity of performance standards in reporting assessment results, it is important that the NAEP standards be set in defensible ways. Because we have concerns that the current NAEP performance standards (formerly called "achievement levels") are flawed, we recommend that the Governing Board and NCES undertake a thorough examination of these standards, taking into consideration the relationship between the purposes for which standards are being set, and the conceptualization and implementation of the assessment itself. In addition, any new standards need to be shown to be reliable and valid for the purposes for which they are being set.

4. *Connecting NAEP to the larger network of education information:* NCES has the opportunity to make NAEP more useful by both linking it with, and embedding it in, other relevant data sets on educational achievement and inputs. For example, if NAEP can be linked with state assessments in technically sound ways, it can be used as a way to check the validity of achievement trends in the states. Furthermore, if the link is sufficiently sound, schools and districts could link state assessments with national and international assessment results. Another possibility is to embed blocks of NAEP tasks into other assessments (e.g., longitudinal studies such as NELS) as a way to facilitate comparisons between NAEP results and other assessments. Yet another option is to use other NCES data sets, such as SASS and CCD, to investigate and generate hypotheses relating NAEP achievement to data on education inputs such as expenditures, resources, and student-teacher ratios. Although studies using these data cannot be used to draw causal inferences, they could suggest hypotheses to be confirmed in other appropriately designed research efforts. While each of these possibilities is intriguing, before implementation, we recommend the development of standards and guidelines for linking and/or embedding NAEP task blocks to other assessments or data sets, including the validity of results based on such links. Such standards and guidelines will likely be important, because we know from recent research that the quality of a link depends upon certain technical criteria. For example, the two assessments being linked need to be examined for comparability with respect to their content frameworks, assessment tasks, reliabilities, and conditions of administration.

5. *Utilizing technology:* We recommend that a significant research-and-development program be implemented and sustained to apply modern technology to its maximum potential in promoting the overarching goals and objectives of NAEP. There are many examples of how technology, either currently available or likely to be widely available in the next 10 to 15 years, can be used to create and score NAEP exercises. These exercises will allow the measurement of higher-order thinking skills and contributions to group problem-solving in ways not currently available, and at relatively low costs.

THE NEED FOR RESEARCH

Planning a program of innovation suggests the following critical research needs:

1. *Research on Assessing Achievement:* The most important recommendation made in the report is that NAEP employ a broader definition of achievement, one that places great emphasis on understanding and the active use of knowledge. To support this change, we recommend a program of basic and applied research to increase understanding about the following issues:

   ▨ the problem-solving model and its applicability for subjects such as reading, writing, history, the social sciences, and the arts (in addition to science and mathematics);

   ▨ the application of cognitive science to classroom learning—and therefore, to achievement and the assessment of achievement;

- the dimensions or components that describe problem solution (e.g., knowledge and skills, problem representation, rules and strategies, metacognition, explanation, and interpretation), the generality of these dimensions, and the extent to which specialization by subject matter is required;

- the psychometric applications implied by the cognitive process model, in contrast to the IRT model currently used with NAEP;

- the role of social context in learning and achievement, as well as group dynamics and individuals' contributions to group problem-solving;

- performance assessment, focusing on the generalizability of performance tasks under varying conditions of assessment and the impact of guides used to score performance tasks, and the

- empirical evaluation of the reliability, generalizability, and validity of assessment items, in relation to measuring different aspects of achievement.

2. *Research on the Use of Technology in Assessment:* Although the utility of technology already is being realized in many assessment applications, much more research needs to be done to achieve technology's implied potential and to ensure that such applications are not made prematurely. To this end, research should be undertaken in the following areas:

- the use of computers to administer or score NAEP assessments—in particular, the use of adaptive testing applications that can make NAEP more comprehensive and cost-effective, as well as applications that would explicate the strategies and self-regulatory skills used to solve complex problems;

■ the use of computers in group problem-solving and collaborative group-learning situations, including the isolation and measurement of individual contributions to group problem-solving, and

■ the use of videotaping as a way of better understanding how students (including groups of students) solve problems, and as an aid to scoring

3. *Research on the Assessment of Special Needs Children:* The growing ethical and legal concerns about excluding from NAEP children with disabilities and limited English proficiency requires that more research be done on how to include more of them in NAEP. Specifically, we recommend that research continue to be done on:

■ accommodations and adaptations that might be made to NAEP to allow meaningful participation for children with disabilities, including the use of assistive devices for children with physical disabilities; the construct validity of the accommodated assessments; and the range of accommodations over which comparisons with the standard NAEP assessment are warranted;

■ solutions to the problem of valid assessment of students for whom English is a second language, including the use of NAEP in languages other than English; adaptations or accommodations that decrease the non-essential language requirements of the assessment exercises; increases in participation that can be achieved through such strategies; and the construct validity of the resultant scores; and

▨ strategies to address the needs of an increasingly diverse population to ensure that NAEP can assess what children know and can do in ways that do not work to the detriment of those from different cultural backgrounds.

4. *Research on Motivation:* The validity of NAEP results for informing the nation presupposes that students participating in NAEP take the assessment seriously and try to do their best in responding to the exercises. However, there is a definite, if unproven, perception that group scores, at least for older students, are depressed by widespread problems of motivation. Therefore, we recommend further research into the impact of student motivation on NAEP scores, in addition to research efforts aimed at creating assessment conditions that enhance student motivation.

5. *Research on Reporting:* Finally, NAEP must conduct systematic research, related to successful reporting of NAEP, to:

▨ demonstrate that profile scores (where the components would be knowledge and skills, problem solving and interpretation, and performance in groups) can be built in construct valid and reliable ways, and

▨ investigate the cost and effectiveness of alternative formats for displaying and describing NAEP results as these affect audience interest, breadth of exposure, ability to understand results, and accuracy of interpretation.

The Need to Plan

Implementing this recommended program of innovation and research will require substantial planning *prior* to the reauthorization of NAEP in 1998. For this reason, we recommend that NAGB and NCES immediately begin to undertake strategic planning for NAEP, and to involve key stakeholders in the planning process. We also recommend that Congress help underwrite this planning effort by guaranteeing funding for NAEP at least four to five years in advance.

1. *We recommend that NAEP provide a known assessment schedule with subject areas, grades to be assessed, and years of assessment essentially guaranteed* in order for states to take full advantage of NAEP in their programmatic efforts and assessment programs.

2. Better planning is required to protect core NAEP operations from disruptions or from unanticipated and negative effects caused by the introduction of unplanned or untested changes in NAEP operations and methods. *Therefore, we recommend that no change in the design of NAEP should be introduced that has not been thoroughly field-tested as part of an overall assessment plan.* Major changes, such as many of those envisioned in this report, likely will require iterative development of new methods, procedures, and items prior to large-scale field-testing and eventual incorporation into operational assessments.

3. *We recommend that framework development begin up to five years in advance of the implementation of an assessment.* Adequate time must be provided and procedures need to be developed for representing the perspectives of diverse stakeholders, for generating a statement of current and

future knowledge and skill requirements, for designing task specifications, and for empirical tryout of item types before the specifications are finalized. In this regard, *we recommend that at least 18 months should be available for the development of task specifications for each subject-matter area assessed by NAEP.*

4. Because the enriched conceptualization of achievement suggested in this report requires the use of many performance tasks, far more time is going to be needed to write, review, and field-test tasks for future NAEP assessments. To ensure that all these steps occur in a coordinated and timely manner will require substantial planning on the part of the Governing Board and NCES. Furthermore, the entire process should involve advice and review of subject-matter specialists. We commend NCES for establishing standing committees of subject-matter specialists to participate in this process. However, *because we believe the activities of the subject-matter panels are so important, we recommend that the Commissioner appoint their members in order to raise the visibility, legitimacy, and influence of the panels.*

5. NCES and NAGB need to plan for the introduction of new trend lines at the same time that new frameworks are introduced. To accomplish this, *we recommend that when a new trend line is introduced, the old trend line be continued for at least one more 8- through 10-year cycle.* Ideally, we would like to see trend lines run, on average, for 20 years before ending them. As the current NAEP long-term trend results demonstrate, it can take four or five assessment cycles to verify whether changes in a trend line are real or aberrant.

6. *We further recommend that NAGB and NCES develop a long-range plan for overlapping trend lines.* Such a plan requires the commitment to parallel activities that span the time interval

of the individual trend lines (e.g., framework revision, item development, item tryouts, etc.), including trying out any changes in methods or procedures that could introduce assessment error prior to introducing them into the assessment. We suggest that these parallel activities begin roughly five years before the introduction of a new content-area framework.

COMING FULL CIRCLE

As the nation strives to improve and maintain the quality of our education system, it is imperative that we have trustworthy data on whether our students are learning what they need to know to be productive and informed citizens in the 21st century. We continue to believe strongly that the fundamental purpose of NAEP is to inform the public and policy-makers about student achievement in the states and in the nation and to stimulate democratic debate about how to improve the education our children receive. In this report, we have suggested ways in which NAEP can be even more useful in the first decades of the 21st century than it has in its nearly 30-year life. If these objectives are met, NAEP will prove invaluable to those who will engage in the debate about American education, from our homes and schoolhouses to the White House.

FOREWORD:
THE BACKGROUND AND CONTEXT FOR THIS REPORT

SINCE ITS INCEPTION IN 1969, The National Assessment of Educational Progress (NAEP) has been the nation's leading indicator of what American students know and can do. The high-technical quality of the assessment and its independence from education and political pressures have enabled NAEP to monitor trends in education achievement reliably for nearly three decades. Moreover, as the only assessment administered to a large and representative sample of American students, NAEP has tracked accurately changes for educationally important subgroups of students as well as the student population as a whole.

Despite this record, NAEP was little known to either the American public or to most educators prior to the 1990s. Indeed, NAEP results appeared in only a few select national- and education-focused newspapers, and drew little attention outside a small circle of educators, national policy-makers, and academic researchers. Now, by contrast, the situation is quite different. The national education reform movement of the 1980s, the Governors' Education Summit in 1989, and the expansion of NAEP to include state-by-state assessments have pushed NAEP into the national spotlight. Today, the release of NAEP results is awaited anxiously by a host of interested parties, from the nation's capital to state assemblies and local school districts. Major news magazines, as well as local dailies, carry stories of the latest assessment trends, while campaign speeches, from presidential candidates to school board nominees, are peppered with data and inferences drawn from NAEP results.

In less than 10 years, the NAEP program has expanded the number of assessed students approximately four-fold; has undergone substantial changes in content, design, and administration; and has drawn to itself veritable legions of stakeholders and observers. Taken singly, each of these changes represents a notable advancement for the National Assessment. Taken together, they produce conflicting demands, strained resources, and technical complexities that potentially threaten the long-term viability of the entire program.

As we have discussed in previous Panel reports on the evaluation of the Trial State Assessment (TSA), some of the most significant developments contributing to the current strain on NAEP are as follows:

i. Expansion of the assessment to include state-by-state NAEP.

In 1984, members of the Council of Chief State School Officers (CCSSOs) recommended that the law be changed in order to allow NAEP to be used for state-by-state comparisons. This was seconded in 1986, when the Alexander-James Panel, established by then-Secretary of Education William Bennett, also called for the establishment of a state-by-state version of NAEP to allow states to compare their results over time and against those of other states.[1] In 1988, Congress responded to these recommendations by authorizing a state-by-state version of NAEP, on a trial basis, to begin in 1990. In the six years since, state NAEP has become an integral and welcome part of the NAEP program, but not without costs. For example, many more students must be assessed and many separate analyses conducted in order to produce separate achievement estimates for each participating state. This not only has raised the cost of NAEP, but also has increased dramatically the pressure of work on the National Center for Education Statistics (NCES) and its contractors. Importantly, and contributing to both the strains and the benefits of the expansion, state-by-state NAEP has created a new and significant constituency for the use of NAEP results. This constituency, in turn, has its own priorities and needs that impinge upon the design of the assessment.

ii. The inclusion of more challenging tasks.

The Alexander-James report also called for expanded use of challenging performance tasks (as opposed to the nearly exclusive use of multiple-choice items) in order to provide better assessment of higher-order and critical-thinking abilities. This theme articulated well with the vision of professional educators such as those who were then developing the ground breaking National Council of Teachers of Mathematics (NCTM) curriculum standards.[2] As a result, beginning with the 1990 mathematics assessment, the number of performance tasks in NAEP assessments increased substantially. The 1996 science assessment, for example, dedicates roughly 80 percent of testing time to performance tasks. This trend is consistent with current practice in other large-scale assessments, and it augurs well for NAEP's increasing ability to portray the complexities of achievement. Such assessment tasks, however, also are costly to administer and score, and complex to design and analyze, particularly in view of NAEP's scale and frequency. Moreover, there is a paucity of research on the design and improvement of performance tasks, and on the optimum mix of task types to produce effective and valid large-scale assessments.

iii. Testing broader and more representative samples of students, including students with disabilities or limited English proficiency.

Another important theme during the 1990s has been the emphasis on broader inclusion of diverse student groups in mainstream education and assessment activities. This theme has been underscored by the provisions of the Individuals with Disabilities Education Act (IDEA) and by the legislative mandate for high standards for all students.[3] NAEP also has sought to include greater numbers of students with disabilities and students with limited English proficiency. The goal of including students with disabilities is both clear and laudable, but the challenges are substantial. The same can be said of students with limited English proficiency. The Panel's studies found that some students, who had been excluded in previous assessments because of disabilities or limited English proficiency, could have participated meaningfully without modification of the assessment instruments or administration conditions. On the other hand, other, previously excluded students could not have been included meaningfully without special adaptations or accommodations (e.g., extra time, oral administration, large print, or translation to the student's first language). Adaptations and accommodations not only are costly, but, in many instances, raise fundamental questions about the comparability and validity of results. These are questions for which the existing research base provides few answers.

iv. The pressure to make NAEP standards based, even in the absence of nationally agreed upon content and performance standards.

The 1989 Governors' Education Summit was followed by the creation of the National Education Goals Panel and the congressionally convened National Council on Educational Standards and Testing. All provided fuel to the growing standards-based reform movement. In this context, and in view of the fact that trial state NAEP was the only assessment that could provide comparative data on how the states were performing relative to the new, national education goals, the beginning of the 1990s saw greatly increased pressures on NAEP: first, to produce state-by-state results under a demanding time schedule, and second, to do so in a manner reflective of the emerging—but as yet undeveloped—national standards. At a time when there were no agreed upon subject-area standards in place, the National Assessment Governing Board (NAGB), the policy-making body for NAEP, took up the challenge by committing considerable resources, time, and energy to the development of standards-based assessments, and then to the setting of achievement levels to measure progress in student learning. The achievement levels stressed the importance of measuring achievement in relation to what students should know and be able to do.

In consequence, not only has NAEP been influenced by the movement toward rigorous, high standards for student learning, but NAEP's frameworks and achievement levels have contributed to the movement to set performance standards.

v. The desire for international comparisons.

Concurrent with the push for higher standards in the early 1990s was the development of a major International Education Association (IEA) study that, in 1996, yielded results for U.S. students compared with those from 41 other nations. As preparations got underway for the IEA's 1996 Third International Mathematics and Science Study (TIMSS), states began to push for the opportunity to compare their state NAEP results with TIMSS results. TIMSS, linked with NAEP, should provide the opportunity for both the nation and states to make international comparisons. This, in turn, created a drive to ensure that NAEP frameworks and TIMSS frameworks would be sufficiently alike to allow such comparisons.

vi. The desire to link NAEP with state assessments.

With the appearance of state NAEP in 1990, states also developed an interest in creating linkages that would enable them to compare the results of their state assessments with results from state and national NAEP, and NCES currently is working to establish criteria that will allow states to determine whether or not their assessments are suitable for making such linkages. The potential of linking state testing to NAEP has considerable appeal; states want comparisons of their state test results with local measures of student performance and with results from other states, but the burdens of making such comparisons are directly prohibitive.

As this chronicle of recent NAEP history indicates, in less than 10 years, an unprecedented demand for NAEP results has arisen, creating huge demands on NCES and its contractors. The current press for education reform seems unlikely to diminish in the coming years; indeed, the crescendo of reform movements may well increase, and, with them, the central role of assessment results in understanding whether or not the reforms are having an impact on the achievement of the nation's children.

NAEP UNDER REVIEW

NAEP is at a point, however, where critical choices must be made about its future. As a result of the various demands outlined above, NAEP has grown both larger and more complex; it also has become more cumbersome and technically demanding. Reports are taking longer to produce, and costly errors have begun to emerge, suggesting that NAEP may be showing the strains of the many demands being placed on it.

Several efforts have been initiated to review the design, administration, and structure of NAEP, and to recommend changes for the future. Our own Panel has conducted an ongoing review since 1990 that has focused on the feasibility, validity, and utility of the TSA, resulting in a series of reports to Congress with conclusions and recommendations pertaining to many areas of NAEP.[4]

More recently, the Department of Education commissioned Peat Marwick and Mathtech to undertake a review of NAEP's management and methodological procedures.[5] That report made recommendations to improve NAEP's operation in the areas of procurement and contracting, cost allocation and tracking, decision-making and priority-setting, and statistical methodology.

In addition, NAEP's Governing Board recently released a policy statement for the redesign of NAEP.[6] The document lists 31 policies for redesign, encompassing topics from the number of content areas to be assessed in a given year to the development of safeguards to protect the integrity of NAEP. We were pleased to have the opportunity to comment on and contribute to the document as it was being written. The Governing Board also commissioned a group of methodological experts to evaluate the feasibility of the recommendations in their design document, and this group—designated the Design Feasibility Team—produced its own extensive report laying out the technical implications of NAGB's redesign policies.

All these reports provide useful information for NCES and Congress as they consider the reauthorization of NAEP in 1998. Indeed, the overall goal of these documents has been to suggest solutions, building directly on the current NAEP program, that might resolve some of the most urgent problems. However, the documents are primarily tactical rather than strategic, and, while appropriate and useful for the 1998 reauthorization, their solutions are not sufficient for the long term.

We considered focusing a major part of this report on the current NAGB redesign effort, but decided otherwise in view of the large amount of work that is being done already or will be done to help implement this effort.[7] To complement this ongoing work, a more fundamental examination of NAEP's role and purposes is needed. This is particularly pressing because any changes made now in the interest of resolving short-term problems nevertheless will have an impact on NAEP for years to come. Moreover, the needs for education in the 21st century may require an assessment that differs substantially from the current national and state-by-state NAEP in its conception and measurement of achievement. Long-range planning and research are necessary to ensure that future assessments yield trustworthy results, support valid inferences about what students know and can do, and measure the effective use of interpretation, problem-solving, and critical-thinking skills.

THE PURPOSE OF THIS REPORT

Assessment in Transition is an attempt to contribute to this long-range discussion. Prepared by The National Academy of Education's Panel on the Evaluation of the NAEP Trial State Assessment, it draws from the Panel's six years of investigation and four previous reports to suggest ways in which NAEP should broaden its conceptualization, assessment, and reporting of student achievement.

In the Panel's two most recent reports, a set of principles was developed for evaluating the success of the TSAs. These principles, reproduced here in an appendix, stress the need for NAEP to be a national, state, and international indicator, and emphasize the importance of ensuring the quality and utility of NAEP results. In support of these goals, the principles call for NAEP's content frameworks to be comprehensive and to be sustained over several years so that trends can be measured reliably. Additionally, they call for the inclusion of all students (including students with disabilities or limited English ability) to the degree technically, ethically, and financially feasible. These same principles continue to underlie the current report.

Those who are familiar with the work of the Panel, however, will recognize this report as a departure from previous Panel documents because it

- Does not evaluate a specific assessment administration that has been completed already, but rather looks forward to the direction for national assessment in the coming decades;

- Focuses less on the analysis of specific data and more on broad policy considerations, emerging needs and opportunities, and long-range directions in research and assessment;

- Goes beyond the Panel's previous focus on state-by-state NAEP to consider the entire NAEP program, national and state;

- Sharpens its focus to emphasize the core elements of NAEP content and reporting; and, finally,

- Considers a time frame that, although within the scope of reasonable prediction and planning, is significantly longer than those of the Panel's previous reports or any of the other redesign documents.

In establishing our vision of national assessment in the future, we set our long-range sights on the year 2015, two decades hence.

We feel privileged to provide this capstone report, which culminates six years of evaluation of the TSAs. We trust that it will be valuable to those who must plan NAEP's future for the next century.

Bob Glaser   Chairman

Bob Linn   Co-Chairman

NOTES

[1] L. Alexander and H.T. James, *The Nation's Report Card: Improving the Assessment of Student Achievement* (Washington, DC: The National Academy of Education, 1987).

[2] National Council of Teachers of Mathematics, *Curriculum and Evaluation Standards for School Mathematics* (Reston, VA: Author, 1989).

[3] See Public Law 103-227, Goals 2000: Educate America Act, and the pending reauthorization of the Individuals with Disabilities Education Act.

[4] The National Academy of Education, *Assessing Student Achievement in the States* (Stanford, CA: Author, 1992); The National Academy of Education, *Setting Performance Standards for Student Achievement* (Stanford, CA: Author, 1992); The National Academy of Education, *The Trial State Assessment: Prospects and Realities* (Stanford, CA: Author, 1993); and The National Academy of Education, *Quality and Utility: The 1994 Trial State Assessment in Reading* (Stanford, CA: Author, 1996).

[5] KPMG Peat Marwick and Mathtech, *A Review of the National Assessment of Educational Progress: Management and Methodological Procedures* (Washington, DC: Author, 1996).

[6] National Assessment Governing Board, *Policy Statement on Redesigning the National Assessment of Educational Progress* (Washington, DC: Author, August 2, 1996).

[7] For example, as this report is being released, NCES is holding a competition in which bidders will be asked to submit proposals to implement NAGB's policy statement on the redesign of NAEP. In addition, work on the redesign is being done under several existing NCES task order contracts.

CHAPTER 1:
THE CENTRAL PURPOSE OF THE NATIONAL ASSESSMENT OF EDUCATIONAL PROGRESS

CHANGE AND THE EDUCATION CHALLENGE

POISED AT THE THRESHOLD OF A NEW MILLENNIUM, ours is a society characterized by rapid change; from our work environments to our civic culture, nothing seems immune, nothing constant. Contributing to the sometimes small but cumulative changes in our daily lives are such vast forces as globalization of the world economy; technological advances unparalleled in human history; and national demographic, social, and economic trends that we barely can describe, much less control.

In this complex and changing context, it is essential that we continue the current drive toward improving education. Without a better educated citizenry, there is little hope that the United States can respond to, much less anticipate, the changes that lie ahead. Equally essential, however, is the recognition that improvement without redirection will not be sufficient. To prepare our students for the future they face, we cannot simply do *better* than we have always done in the past, nor can our children simply learn *more* of what their parents learned in the past. Instead, we must move beyond previous expectations and current conditions to address two central education challenges:

- *We must redefine education achievement in terms of what students will need to know and be able to do to be productive and knowledgeable citizens in the 21st century, and*

- *We must create the education conditions that will support this vision of achievement for all Americans.*

What is the role of the National Assessment in addressing these challenges? Can it contribute to development of an educated citizenry prepared for the 21st century? How will it need to be changed in order to do so effectively? What research will be required to produce a NAEP that is well informed by modern understanding of human learning and development? In this chapter, we discuss the first two of these questions: the role and contributions of NAEP to education improvement. The remainder of the report focuses on the kinds of changes needed if NAEP is to fulfill its central purpose.

WHAT SHOULD NAEP'S PURPOSE BE IN THE COMING DECADES?

As the nation continues to debate the quality and direction of our education system, *the fundamental question behind the discussion must be: are our children learning what they need to learn to be productive and informed citizens in the 21st century?* For more than 25 years, NAEP has provided dependable, valid, and reliable data about what the nation's students know and can do. Furthermore, because of its sampling design, NAEP is the only nationwide assessment that provides information in a manner applicable to all students. NAEP is therefore uniquely positioned to contribute to the debate about needed changes in American education. For this reason, *we believe that the fundamental purpose of NAEP should be to inform the public and policy-makers about student achievement trends in the nation and the states. It should do so in a manner that stimulates democratic discussion and debate, and leads to informed decision-making for American education.*

This definition is consistent with the principles established for NAEP at its outset. Going back to NAEP's very first assessment, there was "widespread and long-standing agreement that the purpose [of NAEP] is to contribute to the improvement of education through the process of providing policy-makers, educators, and the public with better information about student achievement."[1]   The first staff director of NAEP, Frank Womer, reflected this sentiment in a 1970 NAEP publication:

> The ultimate goal of National Assessment is to provide information that can be used to improve the educational process, to improve education at any and all levels where knowledge will be useful about what students know, what skills they have developed, or what their attitudes are.[2]

A second and related goal, identified by the *P* (Progress) in NAEP, has been to measure *trends* in achievement. Thus, a recent review of the history of NAEP states "The goal of NAEP [is] to report what the nation's citizens know and can do and then to monitor changes over time."[3]   It is by holding steady to these first principles—producing reliable and valid information, and using that information to track trends in education achievement—that we can redesign NAEP best to face the potentially sweeping changes of the next century.

Although straightforward, these goals will not be easy to achieve. To do so, NAEP must maintain a long time horizon by both anticipating future needs and planning a program that builds in innovation, and ensuring the stability required for reliable trend measurement. Success also will depend on maintaining focus: concentrating on NAEP's fundamental purpose, while guarding against incompatible or secondary demands that could erode NAEP's capacity.

WHICH DEMANDS IS NAEP LIKELY TO FACE IN THE FUTURE?

The reform emphasis on challenging content and performance standards, and raising student achievement has intensified interest in assessment generally, and in NAEP in particular. Because NAEP is viewed as a model of large-scale assessment, and because the machinery is already in place to collect NAEP data for large samples of students, an increasing number of educators and policy-makers are looking to NAEP to perform new, assessment-related functions. In addition to NAEP's established function as an independent national and state indicator of what students have learned at different ages or grades, additional—and potentially conflicting—demands for NAEP are likely to be made as we enter the next century.

REPORTING NAEP RESULTS AT THE DISTRICT AND SCHOOL LEVEL

With NAEP well established at the national and state level, calls for NAEP to report at the district and school level have begun. In the 1994 NAEP reauthorization, Congress opened the door to reporting NAEP results at these levels on a trial basis, with the cost for doing so borne by local entities.[4] One district,

Milwaukee, availed itself of this opportunity as part of the 1996 assessment, and there is every reason to believe that the press for district- and school-level NAEP data will expand in the future.

Districts and schools likely will want to make both across-time and across-level comparisons with other schools and districts, with their state averages, with the nation, and with other nations. However, they also may want to use NAEP results in ways that make unwarranted inferences and are not, therefore, legitimate. Thus, as stated in our previous reports, we urge careful consideration and evaluation of the negative consequences that could result in reporting NAEP results below the state level.[5] Districts and schools may, for example, want to use NAEP for direct accountability purposes. With accountability comes high stakes, and, just as too often happens with state assessments, teachers, inappropriately, may tend to narrow instruction to teach to the test. This, in turn, could lead to inflated notions of student achievement because students could learn to do better on the specific types of items that appear on the assessment without improving general skills. NAEP reading results, for example, might generalize no longer to overall reading skills or to reading results as measured by another test. Should NAEP become widely corrupted in this manner, its usefulness for *any* purpose would decrease.

Additionally, moving the assessment below the state level would create another group of stakeholders for NAEP results—stakeholders who likely will want a say in policy and practical matters related to the governance and implementation of the assessment. As we noted in our evaluation of the 1994 TSA, the success of state NAEP, while considerably enriching the NAEP program, has complicated significantly NAEP policy-making, recruitment, and participation. Our evaluation of state-level NAEP, for example, has made it evident that priorities of the state constituency sometimes can differ from those of a national constituency with regard to such considerations as the allocation of resources (e.g., number of grades and subjects in national assessment versus the number in state administrations), state and national samples, the desirability of within-state breakdowns (e.g., at the district- or school-building level), and the content specifications of the assessment.

If district- or school-level NAEP were to become routine and regular, NAEP might well become beholden to the districts and schools whose priorities for content coverage, the reporting of individual student scores, or other assessment characteristics likely would differ from those of national NAEP. Such differences could divert NAEP further and further from its original purpose: to be an independent and comprehensive monitor of student achievement. On occasion, there have been discussions, if not pressures, to allow NAEP results to be reported at the individual student level. The Panel strongly endorses the current NAGB policy against this usage.

SCHOOL ACCOUNTABILITY

A strong thrust of the education reform movement over the past dozen years or so has been the demand that schools be held accountable for the education achievement of their students. This was underscored at the education summit of governors and business leaders of 1996, in which a central theme was "holding schools and students accountable for demonstrating real improvement."[6] Because of NAEP's excellent reputation, we can anticipate many requests to use it as a measure for accountability purposes.

NAEP's overall design, however, is not appropriate for accountability. NAEP assesses samples of students at particular grade levels; when the assessment is repeated, new samples of students at the same target grade levels are tested. This type of design, referred to as cross-sectional, does not allow for the clear, "before-and-after" measures required to hold educators responsible for results. Furthermore, when an assessment is used for accountability, it should be necessary to consider inputs as well as outputs, and to assess students with a much greater frequency than that supported by current visions of NAEP.

Finally, NAEP background and teacher questionnaires provide only limited opportunities to control statistically for out-of-school factors that might affect assessment results. This means that changes in education achievement attributed to the school in fact might be the result of some other (uncontrolled for) factor. For all these reasons, the causal links between education practices and student outcomes required for accountability cannot be substantiated using NAEP.

DRAWING CAUSAL INFERENCES

Yet another pitfall for the use of NAEP results involves drawing of causal inferences more generally. Policy-makers, educators, and the public are interested in knowing the factors that influence student achievement. There is a natural inclination, particularly when there has been substantial investment in changes in curriculum, instruction, new standards, and so forth, to relate NAEP achievement results to the instruction factors surveyed in NAEP's teacher and background questionnaires in order to draw inferences about what works and what fails to work in one's state, district, or school.

Unfortunately, NAEP is not suitable for drawing strong inferences about which factors or variables account for education achievement. A correlation of student achievement on NAEP with data about instruction practice obtained from the teacher or student background questionnaire does *not necessarily* imply a causal relationship. The 1994 NAEP reading results, for example, showed that fourth-grade students who had received more than 90 minutes of reading instruction a day actually performed more poorly than students who had received less instruction. In this case, the fallacy is easy to spot. The low-performing students undoubtedly were receiving more hours of instruction because they had not yet mastered the basics of reading; their poor performance was not *caused* by the additional reading instruction. A similar example appeared in a recent article in *Education Week* with the headline, "Geography Courses Have Little Effect for Seniors, Final NAEP Report Says." The article begins, "High school seniors who were not taking a geography course outscored those who were on the 1994 national assessment in that subject."[7] This, of course, is counterintuitive to what we know and understand about the effects of classroom learning, and offers a prime example of how dangerous it can be to draw causal inferences and report them without further analyses. In this case, there are various factors that could account for this finding, including differences in student ability among those opting to take geography in their senior year (a caveat mentioned in the article), and the extent of their prior study of geography.

Although strong conclusions about causality are thus beyond NAEP's scope, an entirely appropriate and useful role for NAEP results is to generate hypotheses and provide a preliminary test of hunches about presumed relationships. Such hypotheses and hunches, which relate student background variables, teacher preparation, student-teacher ratio, and so on, to education achievement, then can be followed up by more appropriately designed experimental or longitudinal studies. In chapter 5, we suggest ways in which NAEP could be linked more closely to other data sources to facilitate such efforts.

WHICH CONTRIBUTIONS CAN NAEP MAKE TO THE DEBATE ON EDUCATION CHANGE?

To recapitulate, NAEP, *in our judgment, is best suited to provide information about the achievement of America's students— information that can be used to inform public discussion and debate about education issues.* The nation and the states need reliable and valid achievement results. NAEP—with its frequent broad surveys of core subject areas, large and representative student samples, and sophisticated statistical techniques—is well suited to this purpose. This is not to say, however, that NAEP optimally serves this purpose at the present time.

Indeed, NAEP information, although useful, too often has been of the type that does not inform easily debates about education: particularly debates about specific education practices at the national, state, district, or local level. In the chapters that follow, we examine ways in which this function could be enhanced. We argue that

▦ *NAEP must employ a broader definition of what is meant by achievement than has been used in the past.* NAEP must be revised to reflect more complex, rich conceptions of achievement and to provide the public with more elaborated examples of the nature of student achievement. The public and policy-makers need to understand more clearly what our students can and cannot do, and how their current skills relate to the demands for personal development and participation in an increasingly diverse and complicated democratic society, as well as to the demands of the workplace and higher education in the 21st century.

▦ *Embodying this broader definition of achievement, particularly with respect to measuring "work force skills" as well as "academic skills," will require substantially more time for the development of appropriate assessment tasks and scoring guides than has been given in the past.* Chapter 2 takes up the topic of what NAEP should measure; the theme of *how* it should be measured is reviewed in chapter 3.

▦ *NAEP must improve its reporting and dissemination functions.* For example, the public, educators, and policy-makers could understand better student achievement in science if, in addition to the release of NAEP summary statistics, films of students solving real science problems were shown in forums for discussion about science education, much as was done as part of the TIMSS release in November 1996. A fuller discussion of how to further improve NAEP reporting is presented in chapter 4.

▓ *NAEP should be integrated with other educationally relevant data sets.* NAEP is but one data set in a virtual warehouse of information about education collected by NCES. In chapter 5, we present ways in which NAEP data could be contextualized by integrating information from other NCES data sets.

▓ *NAEP should facilitate linking with state and international assessments* to enable cost-effective comparability of results and trends across nations and states with a minimum of test burden on students and schools.

▓ *NAEP must plan better than it has in the past, and the plans need to be built upon a foundation of solid research evidence.* This is essential if the goals outlined in this report for NAEP in the year 2015 are to be met. To do so will require the development of a strategic plan that includes in its milestones to be reached time lines and resources needed. We stress the need for such research and planning throughout the report, and more particularly in chapter 6.

In short, NAEP must provide information that is seen as so valuable that its results are as awaited and eagerly sought out by policy-makers and the public as are the periodic reports of the Department of Labor on the state of the economy. The data need to be presented in a way that is easily understood and that commands attention. *If these objectives are met, NAEP will prove invaluable to those who will engage in the debate about American education, from our homes and schoolhouses to the White House.*

NOTES

[1] R.L. Linn, D. Koretz, and E.L. Baker, "Assessing the Validity of the National Assessment of Educational Progress: Final Report of the NAEP Technical Review Panel." Report to the National Center for Education Statistics, 1995.

[2] F.B. Womer, *What is National Assessment?* (Ann Arbor, MI: National Assessment of Educational Progress, 1970).

[3] L.V. Jones, "A History of the National Assessment of Educational Progress and Some Questions About Its Future." *Educational Measurement* 25 (1996). An earlier version of this paper appears as L.V. Jones, "The National Assessment of Educational Progress, Origins and Prospects," in *Assessment in Transition: Monitoring the Nation's Educational Progress, Background Studies* (Stanford, CA: The National Academy of Education, 1997).

[4] National Assessment Governing Board, *Positions on the Future of National Assessment of Educational Progress, 1993* (Washington, DC: Author, 1993).

[5] Panel member Gordon Ambach continues to dissent from the Panel's position on reporting NAEP below the state level; he is on record elsewhere as recommending the lifting of the prohibition at the district level, where the size of the enrollment allows sampling comparable to that used at the state level. Panel members Edward Roeber and Pasquale DeVito dissent as well.

[6] 1996 National Education Summit Policy Statement, National Education Summit, March 26-27.

[7] M. Lawton, "Geography Courses Have Little Effect for Seniors, Final NAEP Report Says." *Education Week* XV (40) (July 10, 1996): 5.

CHAPTER 2:
WHAT SHOULD NAEP MEASURE?

AMERICANS CARE DEEPLY about the quality of education their students receive. As a nation and as individuals, we want our children to be provided with an education that will enable them to operate as competent individuals in their occupations, as thoughtful citizens contributing to society, and as responsible participants in their social relationships more generally. We want our children to leave school equipped with "actionable knowledge"—knowledge that allows them to make well-thought out decisions and that improves the quality of their individual lives in realms as diverse as civic responsibility, family, personal health, and cultural appreciation.

As we move into the 21st century, universities, the government, and the workplace all will require that students complete high school prepared to work well with ideas, and to apply their knowledge and skills competently to a variety of situations. Increasingly, the ability to respond ably in a fast-paced, changing environment will be key. Jobs at all levels will require relevant knowledge and skills, as well as the ability to solve problems, often with short time lines. The instant access to news and electronic libraries of information, which are among the fruits of our rapidly changing technological society, also will demand that citizens be able to make sense out of ill-formed, sometimes intentionally misleading, and often unverifiable statements about events and the world. Informed citizens will need to evaluate and come to appreciate positions of advocacy derived from diverse perspectives. The abundance of information, as well as misinformation, will require considerable skill in interpretation in order to sort through and make sense of the multiplicity of meanings and intents. It is imperative, therefore, that tomorrow's students leave school with a solid, extensive base of active knowledge that can be applied to a variety of situations at their offices, in their communities, and in their individual lives.

NAEP's substantial visibility as the nation's report card presents it with an important opportunity to take leadership in educating the American people about the nature of the competencies that our students will need to meet the demands of the next century. NAEP can do this first, by basing its assessments on new, broader conceptualizations of achievement, accomplishment, and competence, and second, by providing specific and compelling examples of the kinds of skills and knowledge our students must have if they are to succeed in the 21st century.

What Are the Education Needs of the Next Century Likely to Be?

No one can say for certain what the education needs of society will be in the next century. What we can say, however, is that the needs almost certainly will continue to change, and, in some cases, rather quickly. One only has to see how computer and network technologies have penetrated modern life in the past 15 years to understand this. The personal computer did not appear in great numbers in education institutions or the workplace until the 1980s, but in less than 10 years, computers have become ubiquitous in these settings. In the early 1980s, network applications, such as electronic mail and file transfer, were found primarily in universities and the military, but today, electronic mail has spread to vast numbers of businesses, and to homes as well. Anyone with a computer and modem can access data resources from all facets of modern life through the Internet for just a few dollars a month.

Technology is not the only place where changes have occurred. Indeed, the conditions of our lives are in flux. Witness the huge changes in family and social patterns that have occurred over the past 25 to 30 years. There have, for example, been major increases in single-person households (which have expanded from 13 percent of U.S. households in 1970 to more than 31 percent in 1994), juvenile arrest rates (up from 900 per 100,000 young people in 1965 to 1,300 per 100,000 in 1992), and married women with children under six-years-old who are working or seeking work (risen from less than 20 percent in 1965 to 60 percent in 1992). Furthermore, the percentage of children living with one parent has grown from 12 percent in 1970 to 27 percent in 1994, and, of those, the proportion who live with a never-married parent has increased by one-half in the past decade (from 24 to 36 percent), while the proportion who live with a divorced parent has declined (from 42 percent to 37 percent).[1]

These many changes are affecting the kinds of skills and competencies necessary for successful and satisfying lives. American businesses and industries are unable to absorb unskilled high school dropouts or graduates the way they did after the Second World War. Rather, since the early 1990s, business leaders have argued that schools are turning out many graduates who are unproductive because they are deficient in basic skills such as reading, writing, and mathematics. These business leaders report spending substantial time and money in remedial education for their employees—providing skills training that schools reasonably should have been expected to teach. In one response to these latter concerns, the Department of Labor created the Secretary's Commission on Achieving Necessary Skills (SCANS) to identify skills required in the modern workplace.[2]

Society in the 21st century will require even more skilled workers and informed citizens than are required today. The demand for persons who can work with ideas and who have the ability to solve problems across a variety of situations will be great. Everyone in society will need to be educated for their positions. In addition to college education, there will be a huge, continuing growth in the broad technical education required for a workforce that depends not only on facts and skills, but also on an ability to adapt as the requirements of jobs change.

The imperatives of our increasingly complex economy already touch virtually everyone. High school graduates who choose to move directly into the workforce must bring job-relevant skills and a willingness to continue their professional development. Students who drop out of school or young people who are incarcerated also must learn skills that will position them to become productive citizens in society. These compelling requirements, coupled with the changing demographics of our nation, present a formidable challenge for our schools to provide all our students with an education that will allow them to compete successfully in the 21st century.

Nor is the economy the only source of modern complexity. The growing intricacies of civic life are illustrated by recent elections, in which citizens in many states were faced not only with the usual array of candidates for office with media-intensive campaigns, but also with an array of propositions, state constitutional amendments, and referendums. Included among these initiatives were many complex social issues such as term limits, gambling, land use, environmental protection, affirmative action, and the right of parents to determine the content and conduct of their children's education. Informed decisions on such issues, in addition to the claims and counterclaims of candidates, requires considerable skill in interpretation of information and perspectives. Furthermore, one reasonably can anticipate that the demands placed on citizens in these regards only will increase in the next century. Clearly, therefore, schools also must educate individuals for civic responsibility: schools must provide students with the knowledge, interpretive skills, critical-thinking abilities, and problem-solving skills necessary for responsible citizenship in a democratic society and an ever-changing world.

In summary, the dynamic, changing nature of society means that facts and skills learned as part of the schooling process will have shorter and shorter half-lives. As a result, *there are many content areas in which the facts and knowledge taught today will be insufficient for meeting society's needs in the future. Instead, society will require individuals who have learned critical-thinking and problem-solving skills in a variety of content areas, and who are able to generalize these skills to arenas yet to be considered.* It also will require individuals to obtain and interpret information from diverse sources representing multiple perspectives.

NAEP MUST EMBRACE NEW CONCEPTIONS OF ACHIEVEMENT

NAEP always has been a leader in assessment. Beginning with the 1990 assessment in mathematics and continuing up to and including the 1996 science assessment, NAEP has moved significantly from an assessment that consisted largely of multiple-choice items to one that has included increasing numbers of performance tasks intended to measure more complex, higher-order thinking skills. This change is certainly an important step. If the demands of the 21st century are to be met however, *NAEP must evolve even further as an assessment of students' capacity to reason and construct meaning in the content areas NAEP assesses.* As part of this evolution, NAEP also must take into consideration the kinds of concerns that led to the SCANS work. That is, NAEP should strengthen assurance that school-leavers at all levels of education are entering the workforce with problem-solving and higher-order thinking skills, integrated with basic literacy and mathematics skills. To do this, NAEP will need to assess critical-thinking and problem-solving skills across the full range of an achievement domain, and not only among exceptional students.

EARLIER UNDERSTANDINGS ABOUT THE NATURE OF ACHIEVEMENT

Contemporary understandings of achievement and competence have changed substantially since NAEP began, more than 25 years ago. Earlier conceptions assumed that knowledge was a collection of discrete facts and specific procedural rules, and that achievement could be measured by determining the amount of a given domain of knowledge that had been learned. Furthermore, growth in achievement was viewed as linear; achievement could be ranked from low to high, beginning with the amount of knowledge accrued and progressing to the use of that knowledge for thinking.

Now, however, we understand that these models fail to fit the way that children learn. To be concerned with mathematical facts, for example, before moving on to thinking with numbers, is to turn the natural learning process upside-down. Young children learn to judge and compare quantities and to express concern about increasing and decreasing amounts in everyday activities. It is in the context of these activities that they begin to use conventional mathematics procedures in meaningful situations.

Linear, additive models of achievement led to assessments based on many discrete items, often multiple choice or fill-in-the-blank. Thus, in the mathematics domain, one would assess the ability to do addition and subtraction, followed by multiplication and division, followed by algebra, and so on.

Such assessments could generate highly reliable scores, but the scores might be valid for only a particular kind of knowledge— the recall of facts and the straightforward application of a set of rules. No measure could be provided of the ability to generalize this knowledge to problem solutions in different contexts (e.g., real-world applications).

Contemporary conceptions about the acquisition of knowledge and competence have expanded to emphasize the dynamic, reciprocal relationship between basic facts and skills on the one hand, and interpretation and problem-solving abilities on the other. Assessments also must expand to capture this understanding. NAEP already has begun to move in this direction, but, in common with most other current assessment efforts, has found itself hampered by basic structural features of testing methodology that are tied to earlier, linear models of achievement. Current plans for the redesign of NAEP, as important as they are, still do not take adequate account of the significance that modern understanding of achievement and components of subject-matter competence must have for NAEP as we enter the next century.

CONTEMPORARY VIEWS ON THE COMPONENTS OF ACHIEVEMENT

In the course of the 20th century, the study of human cognition has resulted in a steady increase in our understanding of how knowledge is acquired, remembered, and utilized. Particular attention has been paid to the ways in which people express what they know, and the qualities of knowledge and cognition that develop in the course of education and experience. Thus, contemporary knowledge about achievement and competence provides useful insights into how effective problem-solving and complex understanding is achieved, and explicates the characteristics that distinguish between competent and less competent solutions, explanations, and interpretations.

These insights are potentially very important for NAEP in considering how to move from what assessment is today to what assessment could be in the year 2015. For example, rich descriptions of the underlying components of knowledge and skills in different subject matters are becoming available that distinguish between levels of education attainment. As research-and-development on NAEP proceeds, we can expect to describe and report achievement in terms of the cognitive processes of beginning and advanced performance, and to be able to indicate the components of understanding that license problem solution, interpretation, and the construction of meaning from information.

These conceptions of achievement do not displace knowledge of basic skills, facts, and concepts. Rather, they incorporate knowledge of basic skills, facts, and concepts as one dimension of achievement. What we are suggesting, therefore, is a broadening of the meaning of the *E* (Educational) in NAEP.

In general, attainment in various areas of study involves the use of cognitive abilities or competencies that can be assessed to indicate the growth of achievement. In the course of schooling, students develop cognitive competencies that are particularly relevant to specific subject matters, and that also can be generalized to new situations and experiences, and to further learning. For the purposes of suggesting the richness with which student achievement might be described, we elaborate below on an often studied form of competence that distinguishes students' performances, namely, problem solution or problem interpretation with acquired knowledge.

KNOWLEDGE AND SKILLS

NAEP needs to assess factual knowledge and component skills in a given content area as one dimension of achievement. A complete knowledge base however, as we argue here, is more than a repository of facts, skills, and concepts; it includes also the ability to identify and apply these various components in appropriate life situations. For example, high-achieving individuals are better able to recognize where particular knowledge is relevant and how it should be implemented than are lower achievers. High-achieving individuals integrate knowledge; as a result, competent individuals are able to make inferences from what they know, and to interpret new information. They can connect new knowledge with other usable information and skills, and can understand the relationship of new knowledge to information already in their knowledge base. Less proficient individuals display fragmented knowledge that is more isolated in reference to how it can be understood and applied.

As we have indicated, there is a dynamic relationship between problem-solving in a given domain and the contents of one's knowledge base in that domain. For example, the knowledge and skill base in elementary mathematics includes facts from the domains of number, quantity, functions, space, and so on—many learned through general reading or by rote;[3] but the base also includes knowledge developed as a function of past problem-solving. To see how this applies, consider a high school mathematics student looking at a scatterplot of data.

Drawing on her knowledge of functional forms, the student tries to fit a straight line to the data. She solves the appropriate equations, then uses a related skill to evaluate the goodness of fit by examining the residuals (the difference between the values implied by the straight line function and the observed data at a given point on the straight line). When she finds that the fit is far less good in both tails of the distribution than it is for values in the middle of the distribution, she realizes that her existing knowledge base (of linear functions) is inadequate to solve the problem.

The student next examines her textbook for different types of functions and, seeing the graph of a quadratic function, thinks it may fit the scattergram better than the straight line. A subsequent trial and re-examination of the residuals confirms the superiority of the fit using the quadratic function, and her data problem is solved. As a byproduct, the student has learned about the shape of quadratic functions, and this information is now added to her knowledge base.

This example makes clear the reciprocal relationship between the contents of the knowledge base and cognitive skills used in problem-solving. The process of solving the problem required use of the student's existing knowledge of functions, but also generated additional information about functions, which was then added to her existing knowledge base.

The knowledge base in reading involves different complexities than the mathematics knowledge base. For one thing, competence in reading inherently involves knowledge from a huge variety of other content areas such as history, geography, literature, science, and even mathematics. Indeed, one of the most consistent research findings of the last quarter-century is that students' prior knowledge is a powerful determinant of their comprehension. The more one knows about a topic, the better one understands passages containing new information on that topic. Reading competence also requires an integrated knowledge of text forms and skills in interpreting and applying semantic conventions. These skills are crucial for the interpretation of text, and the appreciation of the multiplicity of meanings and interpretations that derive from different perspectives.

PROBLEM REPRESENTATION

Learners build representations of problem-solving situations, mental models that allow them to better conceptualize the solution space and to draw inferences to be used in problem solution. Among competent problem-solvers, these internal representations, or models, are used not only to plan steps toward problem solution, but also to anticipate and plan for alternative outcomes, and then to plan steps to be taken as a function of those outcomes. By contrast, less competent problem-solvers begin taking steps without anticipating how their actions ultimately might lead to problem solution.

In order to move to problem resolution, competent students may use a mental model to reduce the problem to a more simple one, or alter the representation slightly in order to convert it to a familiar one that they can attempt to solve through a set of successive approximations. By comparison, novices are more likely to generate a much more limited, surface feature representation that is of limited value in moving them toward a solution of the problem.

Representational conventions in mathematics include forms of problems and forms of solutions. For example, one common problem form is the word problem. High-achieving students learn to interpret and represent the information in word problems in relation to the mathematical operations used to solve them.[4] One of the most fundamental representations is that of a mathematical function. Other examples include the form of proof that typically is used in high school geometry, and the use of the fundamental theorem of counting in order to determine permutations. Shown in figure 2.1 is an example of how middle school students represented a problem in determining the volume of an object.[5] This question requires students to compute the volume of an irregular rectilinear figure.

Figure 2.1

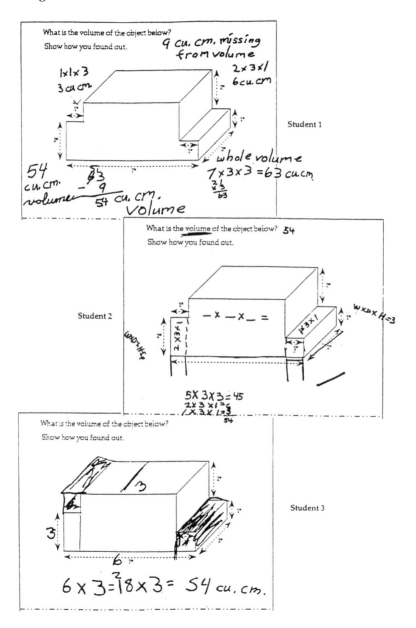

What is the volume of the object below? Show how you found out.

9 cu. cm. missing from volume

1x1x3
3 cu cm

2x3x1
6cu. cm

whole volume
7x3x3 = 63 cu.cm

Student 1

54 cu. cm. volume − 63 / 9 = 54 cu. cm. Volume

What is the volume of the object below? 54
Show how you found out.

Student 2

5X 3X3 = 45
2x3 x1 = 6
1x3x1 = 3
54

What is the volume of the object below?
Show how you found out.

Student 3

6 × 3 = 18 × 3 = 54 cu. cm.

Students must recognize that they cannot use any of the volume formulas they have learned without first representing the figure, the formula, or both. Figure 2.1 contains student solutions illustrating three different representation procedures used to solve this problem.

Student 1 exemplifies a composition procedure, which involves adding components to the original nonrectangular object to produce a larger rectangular object, calculating the volumes of the rectangular object and the added components, and then subtracting the component volumes from the volumes of the rectangular object. Student 2 employs a decomposition procedure, in which the object is segmented into rectangular pieces. The volume of the whole object is calculated as the sum of the component volumes. Student 3 uses a translation procedure, indicated by shading. Here representation entails segmenting the object into component objects and rearranging the components to create a rectangular object whose volume can be calculated.

Consider now how problem representation occurs in reading. Just as mathematics includes forms of problems, there are various forms of text structure that facilitate comprehension in reading. For example, history employs time-ordered, synchronized structures. By contrast, zoology tends toward description and categorization. By middle school, students' ability to represent text includes various genres such as narratives, poetry, and expository text.

A reader forms a representation of the text's message and continuously updates it as subsequent text information is encountered. This representation is formed by attending to the information in the text and combining it with knowledge of word meanings and language conventions, knowledge about the form of texts and genres, and general knowledge related to the content. In the course of reading, this representation guides the reader's interpretation of the meaning of the text.

To summarize, competent learners begin the process of problem solution or problem interpretation by building mental models. These models are used to both simplify the problem and plan steps to solve it.

The Use of Strategies

Competent problem-solvers have a tool chest of efficient strategies and heuristics (e.g., rules of thumb) to draw from when their knowledge base does not prove adequate for solving a particular problem by rote. In solving a problem, for example, a student may try a strategy known to have worked in previous problem-solving situations. By contrast, a less competent student is likely to try a strategy that is inappropriate for the problem at hand, or to misapply a potentially effective strategy.

A broad array of problem-solving strategies exists in mathematics. Some, such as the strategy of narrowing the problem space, or estimating, are applicable to specific situations. For example, suppose one goes into the grocery store with a $20 bill and wants to be certain that the items purchased total no more than $20. To use an estimation strategy, one rounds up each item purchased to the nearest dollar and cumulates the total as items are added to the basket. The price of olive oil is rounded from $5.79 to $6.00, capers from $3.42 to $4.00, for a total of $10, and so on.

Other strategies are more general, such as looking for similarities. As an example, consider the problem of fitting a function to a scatterplot, discussed in the "Knowledge and Skills" section above. The next time our student sees data arrayed that have a single curve or bend in them, she is likely to see the similarity and understand that the data might be fit with a quadratic function.

Strategies in reading include the device—used extensively by all competent readers—of constantly building and revising a model of what the text "means" at every stage of the passage. Good readers develop an initial interpretation of a text, and then try that interpretation on as the reading of the passage continues. They ask themselves how the interpretation fits within their current knowledge base and how someone with a different background would take a different perspective. New information can open up new interpretations that in turn may require a revision of the meaning of the totality of the text, and so on. By contrast, poor readers may develop an initial interpretation they maintain throughout the text, even if it is not adequate to interpret the entire text.

Current models of reading emphasize that successful reading is a constructive endeavor in which readers actively make sense of information in text.[6] Less adept readers tend to take a less active role in the reading process, and inexperienced readers are less likely to note inconsistencies in the content of their information. Skills involved in making text understandable include questioning and reflecting on what an author of a text is trying to say. In making meaning, students can direct their activity toward making sense of the ideas in the text in the context of their thoughts. They also can collaborate with others in the construction of meaning.

In summary, good problem-solvers approach problems with an armamentarium of strategies—strategies that have proven effective in similar problem-solving situations in the past.

SELF-REGULATORY SKILLS

Poor problem-solvers will persevere long after an approach clearly has failed or will pursue one approach through to the end without monitoring to determine whether or not the approach is likely to be effective. Competent problem-solvers, by contrast, develop a set of cognitive skills used to provide oversight, regulation, and, when needed, corrective action for their performance. They determine whether a given strategy appears to move a problem solution forward or not. They also double-check their logic and review steps already taken. With practice, these skills become an integrated part of problem-solving, and the hallmark of high achievers is the appropriate allocation and management of resources (e.g., time) in problem-solving.

In mathematics, self-regulatory skills include planning tasks to be performed, and, after execution of the task has begun, making corrective judgments in response to feedback associated with one's problem-solving attempts.[7] Finally, solutions are double-checked for accuracy, including solutions associated with interim steps. Skills in estimation are used to check the reasonableness of the answer.

Good readers monitor themselves by asking questions such as "Am I understanding this?" They also know how to draw on their knowledge base to revise meaning when their initial constructs fail. In order to test the adequacy of the meaning developed, they use a range of strategies to see whether they are comprehending the text or not. If not, repair strategies include searching the text for answers to specific questions, general rereading, seeking additional information from other sources, including reference materials (e.g., a dictionary or an encyclopedia), or consulting others presumed to be more knowledgeable about the text. Good readers also come to recognize the texts that can be read rapidly (e.g., reading a Stephen King novel), as well as those that need to be read more slowly and with greater attention to comprehension (e.g., reading *Scientific American*).

A reading program for less than successful readers has been developed that focuses on the use of self-regulatory strategies as a way to monitor progress toward comprehension and understanding.[8] The strategies include questioning or posing questions about the main content of the paragraph, clarifying or attempting to resolve misunderstandings, summarizing or reviewing the gist of the text, and predicting or anticipating future content. Over time, and with practice, students learn to manage these self-regulatory activities on their own with little conscious effort.

EXPLANATIONS

With well-formed, integrated knowledge structures, competent learners are able to draw on their knowledge to *explain* concepts and principles, provide principled justification for steps taken in problem-solving, and draw correct inferences in other problem-solving situations. The explanations of less competent problem-solvers, by contrast, are not compelling. They often offer simple assertions or describe the steps they took without being able to justify them.

In mathematics, students can provide clear explanations of their understanding by showing the steps they have taken in solving a problem or by providing a verbal description of these steps. For a certain class of problems, good explanations begin by stating assumptions and showing the general model that will be used to solve the problem. This is followed by a description of the algorithms or rules applied in order to move from the model to the solution of the problem. Where inferences are drawn, the basis for them is made clear. Advanced understanding is demonstrated when explanations include generalizations to different or novel problems. Figure 2.2 illustrates a middle school student's ability to interpret and integrate the information given in a graph, and to use that information to write a short story.[9]

Figure 2.2

Use the following information and the graph to write a story about Tony's walk.

At noon, Tony started walking to his grandmother's house. He arrived at her house at 3:00. The graph below shows Tony's speed in miles per hour throughout his walk.

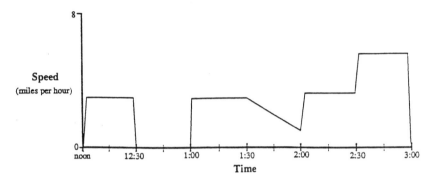

Write a story about Tony's walk. In your story, describe what Tony might have been doing at the different times.

Tony left his house at noon. From noon to 12:3 he was walking about 3½ miles per hour because he was trying to catch ants. At about 12:30 Tony stopped to rest and eat lunch. Then at 1:00 he started walking again, he was walking about 3½ miles per hour until about 1:30 because he was daydreaming. At 1:30 he saw five birds hopping along the sidewalk so he watched them while he was walking which slowed him down a little. Then at 2:00 he finally caught up with his regular pace until 2:30 when he realized the time then he ran the rest of the way.

Similarly, the explanations of good readers involve expositions of the content and processes of reasoning: underlying assumptions, discussions of the nature of the evidence being used to warrant claims (e.g., knowledge about an author's historical or personal context that might explain particular points of view or approaches to character development), intertextual connections with other texts by the same author or of the same period, and depictions of strategies used to overcome blocks in comprehension. In both mathematics and reading comprehension, explanations represent an attempt by learners to complement valid conclusions by "showing their work" so that others are aware of the reasoning that led them to those conclusions.

INTERPRETATION

Individuals develop abilities to interpret information about events around them, about themselves, and about information obtained from reading or other sources. They see things in different perspectives, and take different points of view on the basis of which they discuss, act out, or sketch a situation. In many school subject areas, active knowledge involves interpreting and making sense of various sources and experiences. For example, learning history in high school involves using texts and other documentary material. The student learns to make meaning from the information available in the story.

In addition to historical facts and events, competence in historical thinking involves representation of the situation, evaluation of claims and arguments as distinct from factual assertions, and construction of one's interpretation of the events. Representation occurs as students attempt to understand the relationship of claims, evidence, and sources of information. The students also can consider the differences between the perspective of the author and the perspective that they themselves bring to understand the text. Competence is displayed in the course of learning by recognizing and describing the controversial aspects of the story, the claims of different historical depictions, and the relationships between them.

These evaluation and representation processes that contribute to interpretation skills represent a cognitive competence that can be assessed as an outcome in the study of history and other subjects, in addition to the student's knowledge of facts and events.[10] An example of interpreting different perspectives in a NAEP assessment situation is illustrated in figure 2.3. The task, which appeared in the 1994 geography assessment and addressed the theme of environment and society, asks students to describe how environmental issues are viewed differently by people in different circumstances.

Interpretation in reading means developing a rich web of meaning in which new knowledge becomes part of an available background. Developing an interpretation occurs as readers extend their initial impressions and develop more thought-through and elaborated understandings. As in history and other subject matters, interpretation in reading and writing requires students to think about more than one aspect of the text. This often involves reflecting on changes over time, exploring motivations, analyzing characters, and seeking explanations. Successful readers can link information across parts of a text, as well as focus on specific information.

Figure 2.3

Bas/Rothco

Environmental issues are viewed differently by people in different circumstances. Explain how the artist makes this point in the cartoon.

_____

_____

_____

_____

Geography Content Area: Environment and Society

Grade 12	Percentage "Essential" or "Complete" Within Achievement Level Intervals			
Overall Percentage Essential or Complete	Below Basic 269 and below*	Basic 270-304*	Proficient 305-338*	Advanced 339 and above*
40 (1.7)	7 (1.6)	40 (2.4)	71 (3.6)	***

*NAEP geography composite scale range. *** Sample size insufficient to permit a reliable estimate (see Appendix A).
The standard errors of the estimated percentages appear in parenthesis. It can be said with 95-percent certainty that, for each population of interest, the value for the whole population is within plus or minus two standard errors of the estimate for the sample.

Figure 2.3 (cont)

Sample Response (Score of 3):

Environmental issues are viewed differently by people in different circumstances. Explain how the artist makes this point in the cartoon.

> The man chopping the tree is riding a mule. The man telling the other man not to chop down the tree is in an automobil and is causing Pollution. In a way they are both hurting the ozone.

A **Complete** response (score of 3) mentions two different views (developed versus developing) and refers to trees and car pollution. An appreciation of tension may or may not be present. Or, the response implies or states the hypocrisy that exists and talks about the tree or the car.

Sample Response (Score of 4):

Environmental issues are viewed differently by people in different circumstances. Explain how the artist makes this point in the cartoon.

> The artist says that developed countries are condening underdeveloped countries for cutting down tree because it adds to the green house effect. But the developed countries are driving cars and polluting the atmosphere. The artists are saying the developed countries are hipocrits.

An **Essential** response (score of 4) discusses the environmental issues, tension (implied or stated between the two worlds), hypocrisy (not absolutely necessary if tension is clearly discussed), and two different viewpoints (developed versus developing). The discussion must be at the national level.

The Role of Social Context

Both social interaction and social context more generally can have effects on an individual's performance. Individuals develop competence in solving problems that arise in community and group participation. In cooperation with others, students build and use knowledge resources as they engage in meaningful learning.

In these social or team settings, a significant aspect of learning that can be assessed is students' ability to recognize and adopt the criteria of competence they see in others, and to use this information to judge and perfect the adequacy of their own performances.

The problem-solving ability of groups is becoming increasingly important in contemporary society. Not only will teamwork be important in the workplace in the 21st century, but our future as a democratic society will depend on the ability of our citizens to be effective in voluntary organizations, on school boards, as members of political parties, and as family members. Competence in working with groups can be represented in assessment in at least two ways: first, by using preassessment activities engaged in by groups of students, followed by individual work on assessment tasks, and second, by assessing individual contributions to group activities. More research is needed, however, to develop assessment methods that accurately reflect the effect of group contexts on individual problem-solving activities.

Summary

To summarize to this point, during the last decade, NAEP has been moving away from assessing primarily knowledge of facts and skills. Although we applaud this effort, NAEP needs to embrace an even more comprehensive view of assessment in the next century. Studies in human cognition have examined the differences between people who have learned to be competent in solving problems and performing complex tasks, and beginners who are less proficient. When learning a new subject matter, both children and adults can develop special features of their knowledge that contribute to their ability to use it well. Key among these features are integrated knowledge, so that students can think and make inferences with what they know, and usable knowledge, knowledge that is not mere factual information, but information that can be used in appropriate situations. Knowledge of this sort enables students to represent problems accurately with respect to underlying principles, select and execute goal-directed solution strategies based on an understanding of the task, monitor and adjust their performance when appropriate, offer coherent explanations and justifications, and interpret and make meaning of information.[11]

Finally, to reiterate a central point of the discussion, modern understanding of the acquisition of competence recognizes the importance of the interactions between the more cognitively complex aspects of achievement and one's capacity to build the knowledge base. In mathematics, for example, if a student does not learn how to think about situations mathematically, any computational skills are of little use and unlikely to be employed. Similarly, in reading, if a student thinks that the task is to recognize and pronounce words, she is unlikely to learn much from the text being "read."[12] In our view, *proficient achievement involves a reciprocal relationship between the contents of the knowledge base and the "higher-order," cognitive aspects of achievement.*

NAEP MUST BE COMPREHENSIVE

NAEP is the leading indicator of education achievement in the nation and the states. For this reason, it is crucial that NAEP be a *comprehensive* assessment. NAEP must be both present- and future-oriented. Consequently, to be comprehensive in the 21st century, NAEP must incorporate in its frameworks the kinds of knowledge and skills that citizens will need in the 21st century in order to make sensible decisions for themselves and to be able to carry out their responsibilities in a democratic society.

In this report, we present a possible picture of the type of achievement needed to meet the challenges of the 21st century, arguing for a broader definition of achievement than NAEP currently employs. The definition of achievement developed above contains essentially three components: knowledge of skills and facts, higher-order thinking skills that make possible the appropriate application of knowledge, and achievement in group problem-solving situations. NAEP, however, needs to be comprehensive in other ways. In our recent report on the 1994 reading trial state assessment, we argued that NAEP needs to assess the full range of students.[13] NAEP, in the year 2015, will need to utilize assessment conditions and requirements that allow students *at all ability levels* to demonstrate their capabilities with respect to each of these components. *Thus, the assessment of the "the full range of student ability" has a richer, more complex meaning with the introduction of a broader notion of achievement.*

A NOTE ABOUT INCLUSION

In our previous reports, we have taken strong stands on the need for full inclusion. We have argued forcefully for the assessment of *all* children to the degree practicable, including those with limited English proficiency and those with physical and mental disabilities. We have not repeated the arguments for inclusion per se in this report. However, the argument made above for a comprehensive assessment is intended to imply that NAEP assessments, in the year 2015, should include tasks that are comprehensive with respect to achievement and that will assess fairly students with disabilities, with limited English proficiency, and from diverse cultural backgrounds. Such assessments may include the use of accommodations if the accommodations can be shown to result in data that can be interpreted validly. The development and validation of appropriate accommodations is one of the major research challenges in moving toward the assessment system envisioned for the 21st century.

SUMMARY

The main messages in this chapter are as follows. First, to meet the challenges of the 21st century, a more broad, comprehensive definition of achievement must be employed to assess and teach students than has been employed by NAEP through the present. This definition should include the assessment of cognitive skills as manifest in thinking, the interpretation of meaning, problem solution, self-regulatory skills, and explanation. We included examples of how our conceptualization of achievement can be represented in mathematics, reading, and geography, but we also recognize that the specifics of how to apply this conceptualization to the full range of NAEP-assessed content areas would need to be explored and worked out carefully. In all subject areas, *the changes in assessment will require an active program of research* to ensure that the assessment supports valid inferences about student achievement and trustworthy information about trends in performance. Therefore, *we recommend that NAGB reconceptualize its current definition of achievement to take better account of the range of higher-order thinking skills, as well as basic knowledge and skills, and that it begin to build the research-and-development effort that will map these dimensions onto the various subject areas for which frameworks are to be revised or newly developed.*

Second, it is important that NAEP's content continue to be comprehensive—covering not only what is being taught at a given point in time, but also what we believe children should know if they are to live satisfying lives and make meaningful contributions to community and work in the next century.

Comprehensiveness also requires that NAEP assess the full range of students, including those with limited English proficiency and those with disabilities, on all of the various components of achievement: knowledge and skills, cognitive and problem-solving abilities, and individual contributions to group problem-solving.

Third, NAEP is the nation's report card. As such, it should be expected to measure achievement in the variety of subject-area matters that are important for personal and professional development. This would include attention to workplace-related skills such as those that motivated the SCANS commission, including individual contributions to team performance.

We now turn our focus to how to measure this broader definition of achievement.

NOTES

1 Sources include U.S. Census Bureau, U.S. Department of Health and Human Services, U.S. Department of Justice, and the U.S. Bureau of Labor Statistics.

2 Secretary's Commission on Achieving Necessary Skills, U.S. Department of Labor, *Skills and Tasks for Jobs: A SCANS Report for America 2000* (Washington, DC: U.S. Department of Labor, 1991), and Secretary's Commission on Achieving Necessary Skills, U.S. Department of Labor, *Learning a Living: A Blueprint for High Performance. A SCANS Report for America 2000* (Washington, DC: U.S. Department of Labor, 1992).

3 J.G. Greeno, P.D. Pearson, and A.H. Schoenfeld, "Implications for the National Assessment of Educational Progress of Research on Learning and Cognition," in *Assessment in Transition: Monitoring the Nation's Educational Progress, Background Studies* (Stanford, CA: The National Academy of Education, 1997), 172.

4 J.G. Greeno, et al., op. cit., 173.

5 K. Raghavan, M.L. Sartoris, and R. Glaser, "Interconnecting Science and Mathematics Concepts: Area and Volume," in R. Lehrer and D. Chazan, Eds. *Designing Learning Environments for Developing Understanding of Geometry and Space* (Mahwah, NJ: Erlbaum, in press).

6 I.L. Beck, M.G. McKeown, J. Worthy, C.A. Sandora, and L. Kucan, "Questioning the Author: A Year-Long Classroom Implementation to Engage Students with Text." *The Elementary School Journal* 96 (4) (1996): 387-416.

7 J.G. Greeno, et al., op. cit., 174.

8 A.L. Brown and A.S. Palinscar, "Guided, Cooperative Learning and Individual Knowledge Acquisition," in L.B. Resnick, Ed. *Knowing, Learning and Instruction: Essays in Honor of Robert Glaser* (Hillsdale, NJ: Lawrence Erlbaum Associates, 1989).

[9] The performance task depicted here is from the QUASAR Cognitive Assessment Instrument. Project QUASAR (Quantitative Understanding; Amplifying Student Achievement and Reasoning) is based at the University of Pittsburgh. For more information on this and other tasks, see S. Lane, "The Conceptual Framework for the Development of a Mathematics Assessment Instrument." *Educational Measurement: Issues and Practice* 12 (2) (1993): 16-23.

[10] M.A. Britt, M.A. Marron, and C.A. Perfetti, *Students' Recognition and Recall of Argument Information in History Texts. Annual Report for the National Center on Student Learning* (Washington, DC: Office of Educational Research and Improvement, U.S. Department of Education, 1994).

[11] G. Baxter and R. Glaser, *Cognitive Analysis of Science Performance Assessments* (Los Angeles, CA: UCLA Graduate School of Education, Center for Research on Evaluation, Standards, and Student Testing, forthcoming).

[12] See J.G. Greeno, et al., op. cit., 162-3 for a discussion of this point.

[13] The National Academy of Education 1996, op. cit.

CHAPTER 3:
MEASURING ACHIEVEMENT

IN THE YEAR 2015, NAEP must measure achievement more broadly than it is measured now, and it must measure it well. In this chapter, we examine the relationship between achievement and its measurement, and make suggestions regarding how the various dimensions of achievement might be measured. We discuss ways in which technology might be employed by NAEP in the period between now and 2015, but recognize both the uncertainties in forecasting the future uses of technology and the need to develop a solid research base to support many of the uses we envision. We conclude with a discussion on the importance of measuring the full range of student performance, here too pointing to the potential role of technology.

ASSESSMENT TASKS

Measuring achievement depends on the availability of tasks (items) appropriate to the content and problem-solving processes being measured. Currently, the tasks are developed by the main NAEP contractor, working from the frameworks and performance standards specified by the framework committees, and are classified according to the dimensions specified by the framework. Such classifications are intended to ensure that there are no shortfalls in the coverage of particular aspects of the frameworks or performance standards on the one hand, or over-representation on the other. However, there is no *rigorous*, routine attempt to verify independently the degree of the fit of the tasks to the task specifications, the performance levels, or the framework itself.

In the course of our evaluations of the TSA, we examined the fit of the items to the frameworks in mathematics and reading, but such checks are not done routinely as part of NAEP operations. Our studies indicated that better agreement among raters existed when items were classified by specialty areas within the broader content domain rather than by cognitive processes. (For example, in mathematics, there was better agreement for the classification into numbers and operations, measurement, geometry, statistics and probability, algebra and functions, and estimation than there was for the classification into conceptual, procedural, and problem-solving item types.) Thus, it appears that more work is needed to develop robust classification schemes that capture the essential cognitive features desired of assessment tasks and to describe these clearly in frameworks and task specifications.

As a starting point, we suggest that NAEP move toward measuring current conceptualizations of achievement by classifying assessment tasks according to three dimensions of achievement or ways of expressing knowledge. These include (1) content knowledge (i.e., skills and facts in a given content area), (2) problem solution and interpretation skills (i.e., problem representation, the use of strategies, self-regulation, explanation, and interpretation), and (3) the ability to contribute to group problem-solving.

Although these suggested dimensions are derived from research on learning and cognition, other perspectives and classifications are possible. We submit these dimensions as the most viable starting point, and encourage investment in a program of developmental research that would refine the definitions of the dimensions, and test their utility and validity within the context of a large-scale assessment program such as NAEP. In addition, tasks should continue to be classified according to specialty area within subject for those content areas in which it makes sense to do so.[1] This schema, as it is refined and validated, will provide a useful structure for reporting achievement to the nation. For example, we want our citizens to know whether our students are able to use higher-order thinking skills, and, to the degree that they are, whether and how this dimension of achievement is improving over time.[2]

When the process of constructing assessment tasks is completed, each of the various content specialty areas (e.g., algebra as a specialty of mathematics), as well as each of the components of achievement (e.g., interpretation and problem-solving ability), must be measured by a sufficient number of assessment tasks to ensure generalizability from the assessment to the content area as a whole.

Technology may have a promising role to play in the classification and construction of NAEP assessment tasks in the coming decades. Of special importance is work being done with natural language analysis. Natural language analysis employs artificial intelligence models, into which rules have been programmed, that allow computers to "understand" text. Some of these rules may be complex and include knowledge of domains, and the representation of knowledge and procedures for particular uses.[3] The rules allow one to model, for example, the learner and assess dimensions of performance. Once the rules for classifying the properties of assessment tasks can be made sufficiently clear, they can be programmed, allowing much of the work of task classification to be done by computers. Indeed, for complex analyses, the classifications might be more reliable than those done by hand. The results then could be checked against task specifications that have had the same task dimensions built into them. The hope is that technology could help to remedy a problem we have noted in our past evaluations of the content validity of NAEP assessments: the need for challenging tasks for those students exhibiting advanced knowledge and achievement, as well as for those students currently having difficulty getting onto the NAEP scale.

Obviously, this kind of automation for the development of NAEP's task pool will take time and resources. However, in view of a serious program of research-and-development within the context of NAEP, it is not impossible to have this type of system operational in the next 10 to 15 years. For that reason, *we encourage NAGB and NCES to begin the research-and-development work on the automation of task classification and task production at this time.*[4] *Doing so will increase the likelihood that such a system is fully operational by the year 2015.*

RELIABILITY, GENERALIZABILITY, AND VALIDITY

The tasks chosen for the assessment must generate trustworthy results; that is, they must meet the criteria of reliability, generalizability, and validity. One sometimes hears the argument that standard multiple-choice items are highly reliable and not valid, whereas performance tasks are valid but not reliable. This statement greatly oversimplifies. Achievement, as we have conceptualized it in this report, is multifaceted. Multiple-choice items may have a high level of validity for measuring some aspects of achievement, but not others. The same argument can be made about the use of performance tasks. Indeed, the introduction of performance tasks simply expands the range of issues that must be considered in judging reliability and validity.

TASK TYPE

Each of the dimensions of achievement needs to be measured reliably and validly, and it is reliability and validity that should dictate the type of task employed. At the same time however, the distinctions between task types and what different types of tasks can measure has been overdrawn frequently. For example, it has been argued that multiple-choice items can only get at basic skills and factual knowledge, whereas performance tasks are needed to measure higher-order skills and the process aspects of problem-solving. Although the distinctions are not nearly as sharp as this characterization suggests, different types of tasks do play different roles in an assessment. An appropriate mix of a wide range of types of tasks are needed for a comprehensive NAEP that adequately addresses each of the facets of achievement discussed in chapter 2: knowledge and facts, problem representation, the use of strategies, self-regulatory skills, explanations, interpretation, and individual contributions to group problem-solving.

Because performance tasks are designed to be more representative of typical problem-solving situations or complex interpretive situations, in which one is confronted with conflicting information, they would seem, on the surface, to be more valid for this purpose than short-answer or multiple-choice items. However, as is true of other types of assessment tasks, performance tasks must be evaluated in terms of evidence and analyses based on a program of validation research.

SCORING

Since the validity of results based on performance tasks clearly depends heavily on the guides used for scoring them, it is essential that evidence on the validity of those guides play a prominent role in the validation. The scoring guides and the application of those guides to actual student work need to be examined by a group of content experts and judged in terms of the facet of achievement being measured.

We found, for example, in our evaluation of the 1994 NAEP reading assessment, that the quality of the scoring guides was quite uneven. There were several instances in which the guides were internally inconsistent or poorly aligned with other features of the items. Scoring in several cases depended on the *number* of arguments a student made in support of a position, but the students had not been informed of this in the directions given. Tasks designed to measure "critical stance" were especially problematic. The scoring guides for these tasks failed to reflect the more complex reasoning skills one would expect to see when a reader takes a critical stance.[5] Again, in light of the critical importance of the scoring guides, it is essential that content experts examine them closely to ensure that the scores will be valid measures of the intended facets of achievement.

GENERALIZABILITY

Finally, it is critically important that one be able to generalize from the particular sample exercises used in an assessment to the larger universe of achievement being assessed. One finding that is consistent across subject areas as diverse as writing, mathematics, and science achievement is the relatively large degree of variance due to exercise- or task-sampling. The implication is that a relatively large number of exercises is needed in order to get a good estimate of student performance.[6] Because performance exercises also take longer to administer, their use has implications for both assessment time and cost. *However, when there is no other way to assess certain key facets of achievement, costs associated with using performance tasks are well worth incurring.*

In sum, we repeat that, in each instance, considerations of reliability, generalizability, and validity must guide the choice of item type, and certain types of items appear to be better for measuring different aspects of achievement. Assumptions about reliability, generalizability, and validity, however, must continue to be evaluated empirically.

Assessing the Dimensions of Achievement

We turn now to the measurement of the various facets of achievement identified in chapter 2.

Knowledge and Skills

Although it is necessary to assess a student's knowledge of facts, concepts, and skills, this may not be sufficient for assessing a student's knowledge base. In addition, *the assessment must allow the student to demonstrate that she also knows where and how to apply that knowledge.* Generally speaking, multiple-choice and short-answer questions can be used to measure the facts, knowledge, and concepts in a given knowledge structure. They also might be used to measure whether the student understands the situations in which the various types of knowledge can or cannot be applied. However, depending on the task objective, this latter skill might be measured best by short-answer items or performance tasks.

Problem Representation

Problem representation refers to the ability to construct a mental model that allows one to plan for solving a problem before beginning to implement its solution. This internal representation, or model, is used not only to plan steps toward problem solution, but also to anticipate alternative outcomes and then to plan steps to be predicated on each of those outcomes. In writing, for example, problem representation is demonstrated by the way in which a student constructs an outline. In mathematics, it is apparent by the way in which the student sets up a problem (e.g., what equations are written down). Researchers also can measure problem representation by having students classify problems according to their similarities. Novices tend to classify problems by their surface features (e.g., "it's an inclined plane problem"). Advanced students would classify the same situation as a problem involving principles of motion. Other approaches that may be used to measure problem representation in large-scale assessment situations include asking students to draw pictures or concept maps showing relationships among the elements of the problem, and asking them to describe analogies or similarities to previous problems.

Computers also can be potentially very useful in the measurement of problem representation. As one example, computers facilitate the measurement of response to tasks that use spatial layouts to indicate conceptual relations (e.g., drawing concept maps to demonstrate understanding of relationships and details in a content or procedural domain). Paper-and-pencil technology makes it very difficult for students to do such problems cost-effectively because of the difficulty of making changes to their answers. With the computer however, corrections, reconfigurations, or elaborations are made easily with the click of a computer mouse. Current research also suggests that automated scoring of concept maps using templates generated by experts is viable in at least some subject domains. Although more work and supporting research evidence regarding its validity is needed to develop this technology for routine use in NAEP, it is easy to imagine using it rather routinely 10 to 15 years from now.[7]

THE USE OF STRATEGIES

When faced with problem-solving situations, competent problem-solvers draw on a set of strategies, heuristics, and rules of thumb in the process of developing answers. If one approach does not work, others will be tried systematically until a solution is reached.

The use of strategies can be observed in performance tasks, or students can be asked to write down how the problem was solved. In either case, scoring rubrics might focus on the number and relevance of the strategies considered and tried, and the number of times that failed strategies are repeated. Computer-administered items that track automatically the sequence of the student's efforts offer another possibility worth exploring in this area. Videotaping also can be useful, in that it allows scorers to re-examine the performance, play it in slow motion, and so on, while scoring it for the use of strategies.

SELF-MONITORING SKILLS

Competent problem-solvers monitor their efforts to solve a particular problem. They check to determine if the approach or strategy they are employing is moving toward problem solution or not. They also monitor their interpretation of a situation by predicting an outcome and checking it with consequent events.

The same types of task formats developed for assessing the use of strategies also could be scored for the use of self-regulatory skills. Credit would depend upon the availability of evidence that the student had anticipated the outcome of contemplated events before proceeding to solution of the problem, had kept track of her progress, and had self-corrected as necessary. These and other techniques of self-regulation might be evaluated in small, focused research studies within NAEP that allow for direct interaction with the assessed student. The latter would allow the examiner to probe orally and help structure the student's responses with questions (e.g., "Have you seen a closely related problem? Did you have an idea about how to start the problem?"),[8] and ultimately would provide information that could be used in designing assessment tasks better suited to group administration.

The use of computer technology also has special appeal for its promise as a modality for measuring strategies and self-monitoring skills in large-scale assessment. Technology is in development that allows computers to be programmed to provide *process indicators* such as the length of time needed to complete tasks or parts of tasks. Computers could keep track of patterns that students follow in responding to exercises, including false starts and dead ends, as well as patterns that lead to efficient solutions. By the time of the 2015 NAEP assessment, computers may be able to monitor the way students develop responses to problems, and to do this with much more efficiency and for far less money than the current method of asking students to "think-aloud" in performance assessments allows.

Of course, envisioning potential measurement advances that are made possible by means of computer technology falls short of implementing such a technology; a substantial research venture will be necessary in order to develop and empirically evaluate computer-based measures that support intended inferences about the use of strategies or self-monitoring skills. In addition, it is important to consider whether differential access to computers in instruction confers undue advantage to some students on computer-based assessment measures.

In summary, *it is essential that research on the uses of computers for such purposes get underway. At the same time, the main thrust of the research must remain clearly focused on solving the measurement problems presented by a more comprehensive definition of achievement. The value of technology must be evaluated in terms of its potential for assisting in these problems.*

EXPLANATIONS

Competent learners are able to explain concepts and principles, and to provide their reasoning for the steps taken in solving a particular problem. They also are able to draw correct inferences about how the approach to solve one problem might generalize to other problem-solving situations.

At the present time, explanations can be elicited by extended constructed-response tasks or essays that then must be scored by hand. Current use of imaging technology, however, has improved both the efficiency and the quality of this judgmental scoring of student responses. The technology helps with scoring logistics by making it relatively easy to score responses to one task at a time without rehandling response booklets, and by allowing different raters to access the same responses simultaneously. By allowing raters to concentrate on a single task, the process also hones the accuracy of the scores. Furthermore, research on the textual analysis of student essays is being carried out through the use of language analysis systems built into software. Computerized language analysis may provide a practical means of doing some of the operational NAEP scoring by 2015.

With the technology for on-line assessment that is likely to become available in the next decade, it will be easy to have students write essays on-line. Computers allow students to edit and revise their prose in ways that are not possible with the use of paper-and-pencil assessments of essay writing—a distinct advantage for students to demonstrate their writing prowess. Furthermore, with the addition of more intelligence to the natural language systems currently available, it is even conceivable that computers, in the not too distant future, may be able to check out the logic of the inferences students draw from knowledge structures.

Aspects of achievement may be relatively easy to evaluate based on differences in students' revision processes. A student's representation and perception of the aims of an essay largely determine the nature of subsequent revision.[9] Perceptions of the task can be of a shallow nature or of a global, more meaningful nature. Consequently, beginners and more advanced writers make different kinds of changes in the course of revision. Novices typically focus on the conventions and rules of writing, but more experienced students make many changes, including a significant number that affect the text's meaning. Surface, as opposed to deeper, problem representations characterize beginners' performances. Consequently, beginners work on surface features using words and punctuation. More advanced writers conceptualize the task in a manner that allows them to attend to elaborating the treatment of a point, ensuring the effectiveness of argument structure, and estimating utility of shifts in voice, in addition to checking grammar and punctuation.

Once again, considerable research-and-development work will be needed to evaluate the advantages and disadvantages of having students provide essays on-line. For example, issues of the effects this change might have on the validity of inferences about student understanding, possible differential advantage provided to some students in comparison with others, relative costs, and the validity of scoring will need to be evaluated in terms of, as yet, unavailable research evidence.

INTERPRETATION

One of the approaches used to assess student ability to interpret information from diverse sources is to provide students with a series of documents that contain a variety of information representing different perspectives or different formats (e.g., essays, charts and graphs, records) about a topic.[10] Students are then asked to synthesize the information and write an essay supporting one or more interpretations.

Computer administration would facilitate expansion of the types of materials and modes of presentation that students are asked to interpret. Some current work, for example, is exploring the use of video clips of speeches, news reports, and propaganda that are accessed from compact disks so that students are able to repeat segments of the video as they proceed with the assessment task.[11] Expanding the assessment to include presentation media other than printed text is appealing because it makes the assessment correspond more closely to the major sources of information in the daily lives of students. The influence such an expansion would have on the validity of inferences made from assessment results, of course, requires the same kind of rigorous validation research that needs to be undertaken for other assessment innovations.

INDIVIDUAL CONTRIBUTIONS TO GROUP PROBLEM-SOLVING

Work in the business and science worlds, and the public sector is increasingly being done by teams. Because of this emphasis, there will be more demands to know how students perform in group problem-solving situations. This will require new methods for scoring individual contributions to group problem-solving. One possibility is for group members to rate each other after doing a problem. These ratings could be on a number of dimensions (e.g., contributions to discussions that got the group "unstuck," the number of solutions suggested, the quality of solutions suggested, leadership role, task versus motivational contribution, building on other's ideas), including an overall rating of each other's contributions.

Group contributions also can be rated by outside observers. The National Education Monitoring Project in New Zealand, for example, is using videotapes of small groups of students responding to group assessment tasks to obtain a record of student interactions that are then scored by judges who focus on individual students. Students work in pairs or groups of four. Each student is assigned a particular role in the task (e.g., describing a graph that cannot be seen by the other student, or listening to the description and trying to reproduce the graph). Scores are assigned to target students on an individual basis by judges reviewing the video records using a scoring guide associated with the particular role assigned to the student.

The context of computer-mediated working teams or computer-assisted group meetings might provide another means of assessing individual contributions. Computers currently are being used in several schools on a pilot basis in collaborative learning situations.[12] NAEP might supply a database and then ask students to contribute to the solution of one or more tasks that require information search and retrieval, problem solution, and an explanation of the task. The computer could keep track of individual member's contribution to each of these tasks and, through the use of a predetermined scoring protocol, develop measures of students' contributions to the various tasks.

Considerable research will be needed to evaluate the feasibility and desirability of this or other approaches to assessing individual student contributions to group problem-solving. For example, existing research makes it clear that group composition can have an important influence on performance. This finding clearly complicates the problem of design and must be better understood if valid inferences are to be made from group problem-solving tasks.

Because of the high likelihood that computer technology will be able to move the assessment and scoring of the various dimensions of achievement forward within a decade, we recommend that NAGB and NCES support research on the application of that technology beginning now. Furthermore, we recommend that this research include an emphasis on understanding individual contributions to the solution of group problems, including computerized assessments of such contributions. Finally, this program of research needs to assess that these technologies result in fair and valid assessments for all students.

MEASURING THE FULL RANGE OF STUDENT CAPABILITIES

As mentioned in chapter 2, NAEP needs to measure student performance at all ranges and within each of the various dimensions of achievement. NAEP needs to challenge all students, from the very highest achievers to those currently having difficulty doing any of the grade-appropriate assessment tasks because of learning disabilities or mental retardation.

Technology may be able to help in important ways. Already the technology and software exist that allow computers to track which items students get right and wrong, thereby allowing the computer to determine in real time the range in which a given student is performing on different achievement scales. By using this information early in the assessment, the computer then can select additional tasks for administration that are in the right difficulty range for each achievement scale that is challenging, but not overwhelming, to that student. In this way, each student can perform to her highest level, while the potential frustration due to presentation of tasks far beyond her current reach can be reduced.

Variants on this type of computer adaptive testing (CAT) are already in use on some large-scale testing programs designed to produce individual student scores. One of the potential advantages of CAT in that context is that testing time can be reduced substantially by only administering questions that provide additional refinement to the estimate of the student's performance. That particular value, although potentially useful in the context of NAEP, where the focus is on the assessment of *distributions* of student performance rather than measures for individual students, is not the main motivation for considering computerized assessment. Rather, the primary potential value for NAEP is the possibility that some type of computerized adaptive assessment might allow for the meaningful inclusion of students for whom the current assessment is inappropriate, either because it does not challenge some exceptional students or because it does not include tasks that are elementary enough to allow students experiencing difficulty in a subject area to demonstrate what they *are able* to do.

The Goals 2000 legislation and the pending revision of IDEA require that attempts be made to provide challenging assessments to all students, regardless of ability or native language. The goal of including all, or nearly all, students in NAEP is clear, but the goal also poses substantial assessment challenges. For many of the presently excluded students, some form of adaptation or accommodation in the assessment will be required for them to be able to participate meaningfully. Technology may help with some types of adaptations and accommodations (e.g., by tailoring the reading demands to a student's current reading level, by relaxing time constraints, or even by providing an oral translation of text in a student's native language). Technology, however, cannot be expected to provide a quick fix for all of the conceptually and practically difficult challenges of full inclusion.

Furthermore, finding an adaptation or accommodation that enables a student to understand the task and that also provides a meaningful response does not guarantee that the results can be included validly with those of students who do not have adaptations or accommodations, or even be interpreted validly in the same way. Some adaptations are taken for granted, like allowing students to wear their eye glasses while taking the assessment, and raise no validity concerns. In the case of other adaptations or accommodations (e.g., allowing students extra time to complete the assessment, presenting tasks orally to students, providing translated tasks in a student's first language when other than English) however, it is far from clear what the impact might be on the validity of standard interpretations of results. Validating adaptations and accommodations will require a substantial research-and-development effort.

The lead time to develop and validate the kinds of adaptations and accommodations likely to be required for students with disabilities, and for whom English is a second language, is considerable. For this reason, we recommend that NCES and NAGB immediately begin a vigorous program of research-and-development on needed adaptations and accommodations. As part of this effort, we encourage the explorations of (1) the use of computer adaptive technology as one possible way to improve the measurement of achievement at both the upper and lower ends of the achievement domains, and (2) the development of software that will allow the use of on-line accommodations for special needs children.

ADDRESSING STUDENT MOTIVATION

A serious problem in measuring achievement on NAEP concerns student motivation. Earlier we noted that NAEP is a "low-stakes" examination, and that this confers advantages in that the assessment is less likely to be corrupted by practices such as narrowly teaching to the test. The counter weighting problem, however, is that a different form of bias may creep into the measurement if students are unmotivated significantly to expend effort in answering the examination questions.

The extent to which low-student motivation actually affects NAEP scores is not known. Anecdotal evidence suggests that many of the older students are not putting forth their best efforts, and "one of the most frequently offered theories about low NAEP scores is that kids know the tests don't count."[13] Furthermore, omit rates for constructed-response items have been substantial in some recent assessments, a phenomenon that undoubtedly is related at least partially to the greater effort required to answer this type of question. If, as we are urging, NAEP were to move toward greater richness and complexity in assessment exercises, problems of motivation could be exacerbated.

Some research has been carried out to examine the impact on performance when NAEP items are embedded in a high-stakes state assessment, or when special efforts are made to motivate students using financial rewards, competition, or the opportunity to experience personal accomplishment. Statistically significant improvements were observed under some of these conditions, but the actual effect sizes were small, and they appeared only at some grades and for some subjects.[14] The failure to produce more dramatic results may indicate that low motivation is not a significant factor in depressing NAEP scores, but it also simply may serve to illustrate the significant difficulties associated with manipulating student motivation.

NAEP must therefore include in its research-and-development agenda thoughtful efforts both to evaluate the impact of student motivation and to devise assessment conditions that optimize motivation without threatening the independent character of the assessment. With regard to the latter, an important first step would be to establish methods for matching students with tasks at appropriate levels of difficulty. Students are predictably less willing to expend effort on tasks that are much too difficult, and tasks that are too easy probably also decrease motivation to some extent, as well as restricting the student's opportunity to display the full range of her competence.

Student motivation is not likely to be an easily tractable problem, but some strategies that might be investigated include various devices for raising interest in anticipation of the assessment. These could involve such things as classroom review of sample NAEP items, or a motivational video featuring the President, the Secretary, or some other prominent speaker. In addition, the actual conditions of administration could be modified to increase the likelihood that students would spend time on task. Our previous investigations of the TSA revealed that average scores were slightly higher when the assessment was administered by someone with greater authority in the eyes of the students (e.g., the school principal rather than the guidance counselor). Fully integrating the use of computer technology into the NAEP assessment also could increase motivation through the use of more engaging, interactive problems than are currently possible with paper-and-pencil technology. A further and even greater impact on effort undoubtedly could be made if assessments were conducted interactively and in small groups, so that the student was constrained to engage with the task. The New Zealand National Education Monitoring Project, mentioned above, has utilized small group formats of this kind, and the strategy has the potential for generating rich descriptions of achievement, as well as favorably influencing motivation. Finally, NAEP should give further consideration to the feasibility and desirability of some form of feedback to students on their performance, possibly using released items.

Obviously, a tension exists between some of these strategies, particularly those that would involve small group (or individual) administration, and NAEP's large-scale assessment design. However, it should be feasible to design linked subsamples within NAEP that participate under high-motivation conditions, and then to use the data from those subsamples to estimate and possibly even adjust low-motivation effects on the main NAEP results.

THE NEED FOR TREND DATA

NAEP has been invaluable as a measure of trends in education achievement for more than 25 years. Indeed, one of NAEP's first principles focused on the need for trend data. Although trend data for the nation have been of great utility in and of themselves, data comparing minorities with white students on mathematics, science, and reading, as well as boys with girls in mathematics and reading achievement, have been of special importance, as was pointed out in the first chapter of this report. These data have shown us that, although the gap in achievement between majority and minority students closed somewhat in the 1980s, the gap is reopening in the 1990s. These data also make clear that boys read and write at consistently lower levels than girls.

The measurement of trends requires, however, that both the assessment frameworks and the assessments themselves remain fixed over time. As a result, there is a certain tension between keeping frameworks in place for a long time on the one hand, and the need to ensure that important changes in subject-matter areas and assessment technology be incorporated into NAEP on the other. With the development of national content standards in an increasingly greater number of subject areas, we expect there to be more cross-time stability in curriculum frameworks than there has been in the past. However, there almost certainly will be important revisions from time to time. For this reason, the Panel supports the Governing Board in arguing for a cycle of framework implementation, feedback, and revision that takes place over perhaps an 8- through 10-year period. As stated in one of our earlier reports: "Stability over some sustained period of time is important substantively, technically, and educationally."[15] We continue to believe that an 8- through 10-year cycle is long enough to establish meaningful trend lines, but short enough to accommodate the natural evolution that occurs in subject-matter fields. As described below however, we believe it is desirable to continue trend assessments using old frameworks for a total of approximately 20 years from the time a given framework is initially introduced.

Currently, NAEP collects and reports data on achievement trends using one set of trends that began in the 1990s with new frameworks in mathematics and reading, and a second set of older, long-term trends that go back to the 1970s. In order to reduce costs, eliminate confusion, and test in more subject areas, the Governing Board has proposed that main NAEP become the primary way to measure long- and short-term trends, and that the utility of maintaining the current long-term trend assessments be re-evaluated. Because the long-term NAEP trend studies have produced valuable insights into trends in the achievement of American students and subpopulations of students, we underscore the importance of maintaining long-term trend data in some form. *Long-term achievement patterns of interest (e.g., the opening or narrowing of an achievement gap) may take longer than 10 years to manifest. If a new trend line were to begin with each new framework, then the very meaning of "long-term" in long-term trend could be lost.*

There is also the question of whether the data points for trend lines using the main NAEP assessment can be kept comparable. Our observation of the 1994 and 1996 assessments leads us to believe that the likelihood of keeping the frameworks, items, scoring, and assessment conditions for main NAEP the same during a 10-year period is small. Such tinkering as has occurred in the most recent reading and mathematics assessments could jeopardize the comparability of results from one assessment to another. *To measure change accurately requires frameworks and measures that do not change.* The problem would become more critical if main NAEP were to become the only trend data available if the separate long-term trend assessment were to be dropped.

These issues strongly suggest the need for some mechanism for assessing long-term trends in NAEP that exist along side of, or in addition to, the main national NAEP assessment. One such solution could be a systematic overlapping of trend lines to ensure the ability to track and interpret changes in achievement across changes in frameworks. We are not prepared to say how many years the trend lines should overlap; however, it seems reasonable to suggest that they should overlap for at least two assessment cycles. We have illustrated this in the following figure:

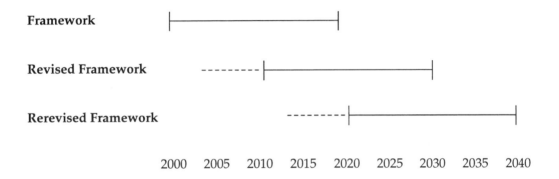

The solid lines represent the period of time a framework would be used to monitor trends. The dashed lines beginning in 2005 and 2015 represent five years of developmental work that should precede full operational use. *That is, prior to the introduction of new or revised frameworks, at least five years of development should occur.*

Summary

The 21st century is likely to put increasing demands on its citizens to be able to react creatively and decisively to changes in our workplaces, communities, and families. Schools are going to have to prepare students with a solid knowledge base and a developed set of cognitive skills that can be used together to access and interpret a wide range of information, and to solve a variety of problems. NAEP can play an important role by displaying the types of achievement that are important and indicating how well our students are doing against these criteria. We are suggesting a broader meaning for the *E* (Educational) in NAEP. Students must leave school with "actionable knowledge"—knowledge that lets them solve a variety of problems in a variety of familiar or unfamiliar situations, and understand and appreciate the world in which they live.

The NAEP of 2015 must assess not only knowledge and facts, but higher-order thinking skills as well—skills that demonstrate a student's ability to evaluate and use information, to draw valid inferences from her knowledge base, and to take the knowledge learned in one situation and apply it effectively in another. In view of the changing nature of work and the growing significance of groups in the organization of work, NAEP also must assess the capability of individuals to contribute to group problem-solving. In each of these cases, we show the important role that modern knowledge and technology might play in the next 10 to 15 years. Overall, we stress the importance of trustworthy, valid, and reliable approaches to the assessment of achievement.

*We recommend that NAEP continue to be a comprehensive measure that incorporates the range of current classroom practice as well as the best theories and data we have to support current conceptions of the nature of learning. We again stress the **P** (Progress) in NAEP—the need for trend data and the prerequisities for valid and* *reliable trends, and, in particular, the need for stable frameworks and items. Finally, we also strongly recommend that, beginning no later than 2015, NAEP trends track the various dimensions of achievement: knowledge and skills, problem-solving skills, including the interpretation of information, and individual contributions to group problem-solving.*

NOTES

[1] In reading, for example, items can be classified by reading purpose (e.g., reading for literary experience); in mathematics, by subarea (e.g., geometry).

[2] It would be useful to have items classified according to their language load. That is, it would be useful to know how much of the difficulty of an item is due to the complexity of the language used in the item. Items classified in these various ways could be useful when examining NAEP in the context of background variables and other data sets at NCES, such as the Schools and Staffing Survey and the Common Core of Data. Such linkages, while far from allowing causal analyses, could well suggest interpretations of achievement results that could be then better examined with other data sets.

[3] E.L. Baker, "Readying the National Assessment of Educational Progress to Meet the Future," in *Assessment in Transition: Monitoring the Nation's Educational Progress, Background Studies* (Stanford, CA: The National Academy of Education, 1997).

[4] Although, off in the more distant future, it is also possible to imagine the use of "intelligent items" at some point—items that are given the knowledge to recognize the attributes the student brings to the assessment (e.g., limited English proficiency) and adjust themselves to those characteristics while maintaining the integrity of the underlying measurement construct. See, for example, E.L. Baker 1997, op. cit., 134.

[5] The National Academy of Education 1996, op. cit., 18.

[6] R. J. Shavelson, "On a Science Performance Assessment Technology: Implications for the Future of the National Assessment of Educational Progress," in *Assessment in Transition: Monitoring the Nation's Educational Progress, Background Studies* (Stanford, CA: The National Academy of Education, 1997), 113.

[7] E.L. Baker 1997, op. cit., 134.

[8] J.G. Greeno, et al., op. cit., 180.

9 L. Flower, J.R. Hayes, L. Carey, K. Schriver, and J. Stratman, "Detection, Diagnosis, and the Strategies of Revision." *College Composition and Communication* 37 (1) (1986): 16-55.

10 The technique is used, for example, in Advanced Placement History Examinations. See E.L. Baker, "Learning-Based Assessment of History Understanding." *Educational Psychologist* 29 (2) (1994): 97-106. It is also a technique used to a more modest extent with pairs of reading passages representing different positions or authors on the Scholastic Assessment Test.

11 Developmental research being conducted by Randy Bennett at the Educational Testing Service.

12 See, for example, A.L. Brown and J.C. Campione, "Guided Discovery in a Community of Learners," in K. McGilly, Ed. *Classroom Lessons: Integrating Cognitive Theory and Classroom Practice* (Cambridge, MA: Bradford Books MIT Press, 1994), 229-270, and M. Scardamalia and C. Bereiter, "Higher Levels of Agency for Children in Knowledge Building: A Challenge for the Design of New Knowledge Media." *The Journal of the Learning Sciences* 1 (1991): 37-68.

13 A. Shanker, "How much do our kids really know?" *The New York Times* (July 29, 1990).

14 V.L. Kiplinger and R.L. Linn, *Raising the Stakes of Test Administration: The Impact of Student Performance on NAEP* (Los Angeles, CA: UCLA Center for the Study of Evaluation, 1992); H.F. O'Neil, Jr., B. Sugrue, J. Abedi, E.L. Baker, and S. Golan, *Final Report of Experimental Studies on Motivation and NAEP Test Performance* (Los Angeles, CA: UCLA Center for the Study of Evaluation, 1992); and H.F. O'Neil, Jr., B. Sugrue, and E.L. Baker, "Effects of Motivational Interventions on NAEP Mathematics Performance." *Educational Assessment* (in press).

15 The National Academy of Education 1993, op. cit., 43.

CHAPTER 4:
INFORMING THE NATION

THROUGHOUT THIS REPORT, we have argued that NAEP, in the 21st century, must be guided by the principles of its original mandate; that is, it must focus on accurately informing the nation and the states about the education achievements of American students. In chapter 2, we laid out important dimensions of achievement consonant with modern understandings of student learning, and in chapter 3, we discussed some of the ways in which the measurement of achievement could be enhanced. Now we turn to a consideration of the ways in which the results of these measures can be brought to life for the American public through rich displays of student performance and high-visibility reporting.

In this chapter, we also discuss a second challenge to successful reporting. Although concrete examples of achievement are necessary in order to ground the discussion of educational progress, meaningful discussion of achievement against standards, comparisons across groups, and trends across time all require the use of sophisticated summary scales and statistics. Unfortunately, studies have shown that even relatively simple statistical representations often are misunderstood fundamentally by important NAEP constituencies. NAEP must, therefore, continue the search for better methods by which to bridge this communication gap and accurately convey its core messages regarding student achievement.

Engaging the Debate

For the past decade, the United States has been engaged in an education reform movement that challenges our schools to attain high standards for all of America's children. In this context, educators, policy-makers, and the public have embraced the use of achievement measures as a potentially important tool for monitoring the progress of reforms. As we work collectively to build schools for the 21st century however, using achievement measures for simple bottom-line accountability will not be sufficient. *Rather, proper stewardship over our institutions of education will demand that the public, policy-makers, and educators also engage in deep and meaningful discussion about the nature of student achievement and the processes of education.* Such debate requires grounding in clear and engaging explications of student performance: a need that NAEP can and should fulfill.

Displaying the Dimensions of Achievement

The scales by which NAEP summarizes its findings must satisfy two important criteria. First, they must reflect accurately the nature of achievement, and second, they must be presented in terms that are as clear and as readily interpreted as possible. As we have argued previously, achievement is dynamic and multidimensional: as students build a knowledge base in each subject area, they also must develop their reasoning and problem-solving skills, as well as a capacity to function as informed and contributing members of modern society. Digesting all of this understanding into simple summary scores of achievement may be useful for some purposes, but does little to educate policy-makers, parents, or the public, or to draw them into the debate about education.

In analogy, the overall ratings, provided by *Consumer Reports,* of automobiles in a certain price range are convenient, but informed decision-making generally requires additional information contained in the subscale ratings for gasoline mileage, handling, rear seat comfort, safety, and so on. Correspondingly, if NAEP is to foster an understanding of how children are performing, NAEP scales must convey the richness of competent performances on challenging tasks. Unfortunately, the present models by which measurement experts summarize across assessment exercises fail to capture the dynamic, interactive nature of achievement. Basic research is needed to develop newer, more accurate models for depicting accomplishment. In the meantime however, NAEP should begin formulating reports that use score profiles to describe performance separately on various dimensions of achievement. As was discussed earlier in the report, it currently appears that at least three separate scores per subject area would be necessary for these profiles—one on knowledge of facts, skills, and concepts; a second to capture the higher-order skills involved in the *application* of knowledge (scientific problem-solving, for example, or historical, interpretive reasoning); and a third associated with performance in groups. Figure 4.1 shows how such a profile might track over time.

Figure 4.1

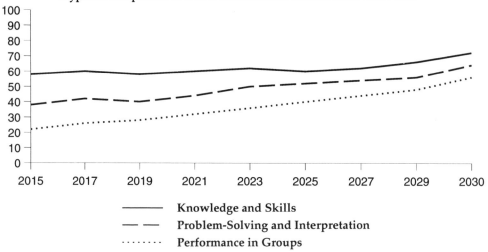

Hypothetical profile of NAEP mathematics achievement trend data

————— **Knowledge and Skills**

— — **Problem-Solving and Interpretation**

········ **Performance in Groups**

In this idealized case, note that the relationship among the different dimensions of achievement changes over time. In 2015, when the trend line begins, average achievement is highest for knowledge and skills, somewhat lower for problem-solving and interpretation, and lower still for performance in groups. Over the ensuing 15 years, performance on each dimension improves, but at different rates. Consequently, by 2030, the gap between achievement on the three dimensions has closed substantially. Score profiles like these would be even more informative if used to convey achievement trends for the various NAEP reporting groups (e.g., grade or race/ethnicity). One might discover, for example, that black students were making significant gains in closing the performance gap with white students when it came to knowledge and skills, yet only holding their own regarding problem solution and interpretation. Such a finding would suggest that students in different racial/ethnic groups were being exposed to different curricula.

We also recommend that the present model of content subscales be continued to differentiate expertise in different sectors of the subject domain. For example, separate subscales might be used (as they are now) to measure mathematics achievement in numbers and operations as compared with algebra. The number and specific nature of the subscales likely will vary across subject areas, but should be grounded in our understanding of competence and be relevant to the ways in which these subject areas are taught in the schools.

In order to make these scales meaningful, the reporting must be careful to explicate both the substance of the scale and the interpretation of performance at different points along the scale. The utility of the current scales for reporting is hampered by the arbitrary nature of the scale values (ranging from 0 to 500), which have no inherent meaning to the audience for NAEP results. An attractive alternative, raised by NAGB's Design Feasibility Team, is to define a domain of achievement associated with each scale, and then to report results in terms of the percent of domain attained.[1]

Even the seemingly simple option of a percent correct reporting metric can be subject to misinterpretation however. Common expectations, for example, that 70 percent is passing, or 90 percent is required for an A, would be inappropriate for a domain of tasks that are designed to challenge students by pushing toward future expectations of what "should be," and, unlike most classroom tests, are not tied directly to the material currently being studied. For all these reasons, even a percent of domain reporting metric requires explanation and exposure to the sets of tasks on which the percent scores are based. It also would require clear explication of what is taught currently in the nation's classrooms. Moreover, if NAEP is comprehensive in defining content domains, it should include in the assessment the union of all available curricula. It should cover curriculum A + curriculum B + curriculum C, yet no individual student taking the test would have had a chance to learn this aggregate version of the domain. For example, a history assessment should include some items addressing the art and literature of a period appropriate for an American Studies curriculum, even though such questions may be unfamiliar to students who have advanced knowledge of economic and political history for the same period. For mastery of basic skills domains, it is reasonable to define mastery by requiring a high percentage of correct items. But as content domains become more complex and inclusive of specialized knowledge, it may be no longer appropriate to expect that advanced students would know nearly everything in the domain.

RICH DESCRIPTIONS OF STUDENT PERFORMANCE

The primary method for explicating the profiles and subscales, and generally infusing meaning into the reporting of NAEP results, however, must rest on a bedrock of clear and tangible examples of student work. A sizable portion of NAEP tasks should be designed—and made available—to demonstrate the kinds of actual performances that we expect of students in classrooms and daily living. This will require a higher rate of item development so that more items can be released to the public, and it also will require that, in some instances, the richness and complexity of student performance be captured using more than pen and paper. Videotapes of students solving problems, for example, would open the doors to innovations in both the scoring and reporting of assessment tasks.

From its inception, NAEP has understood the importance of explaining achievement in terms of performance on specific tasks—tasks whose value could be understood and debated by the public. Over time, these exemplar tasks came to be supplemented by a variety of summary scale scores, and, most recently, performance standards set in terms of the scale scores. Although item exemplars are still used (and widely appreciated) in NAEP reports, much more must be done to display such items in ways that better convey the concrete meaning of the assessment results. Figures 4.2 and 4.3 provide two examples of how this might be accomplished: by providing annotated examples of assessment tasks related to the dimensions of achievement discussed above.

NAEP of the future must do this and more, drawing on our best research about teaching and learning to *inform the public about student achievement* while providing a common body of information to which educators and policy-makers can refer.

Figure 4.2 **An annotated mathematics assessment task of the type that might be used in NAEP reporting**

Here is an example of a task for middle school students that evaluates knowledge of decimals (Knowledge and Skill) and ability to construct a mathematical argument or justification (Explanation). It falls within the content area of Numbers and Operations.

Decimal Task

Circle the number that has the greatest value.

.08   .8   .080   .008000

Explain your answer.

Figure 4.2 (cont)

A conceptual understanding of decimals and fractions is an important goal of middle school mathematics. An understanding of decimals can be applied in problems involving measurement, probability and statistics, and in a wide range of "real-world" situations, notably financial transactions. The National Council of Teachers of Mathematics have stressed the importance of developing a solid foundation in decimal numbers in the elementary and middle school grades, so that time is not spent in later years reducing student errors and misconceptions.

About 59 percent of eighth-grade students circled the correct answer of .8. Of these correctly circled answers, about half were accompanied by justifications that were correct or that contained only minor errors or omissions.

The most commonly chosen incorrect answer was .008000, which was chosen by 27 percent of students. As will be discussed below, the students' explanations revealed possible reasons for these errors.

Students' explanations were evaluated based on both the mathematical bases for justification and the quality of the mathematical arguments that were used. For an answer to be scored as "complete and correct," a student had to compare .8 explicitly with each of the other choices using decimal place value or common fractional equivalence (Justification 1). A justification that was "incomplete but correct" might describe .8 correctly but leave the discussion of incorrect choices implicit (Justification 2), while justifications that were scored as "incorrect" contained a variety of errors (Justifications 3 and 4).

A common error was to confuse whole number place value with decimal place value. A student would circle .008000, explaining that "8000 is bigger than 8 or 80." For some students, this confusion continued even after they had memorized the names of the place values. One such explanation stated that ".008000 is biggest because 8 thousandths is bigger than 8 hundredths or 8 tenths." As students learned more about decimal place value, some still had difficulty considering all four given numbers within a common framework. These students seemed not

Figure 4.2 (cont)   **Four examples of justifications are shown.**

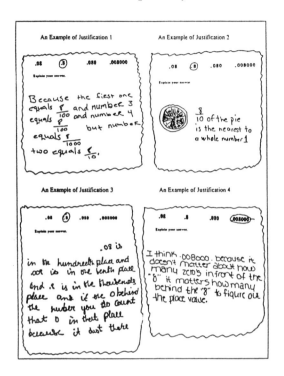

to understand the hierarchy of rules for comparing decimal numbers, and they had difficulty coordinating decimal place values with the digits in the decimal places. Their explanations might display partial knowledge, such as "tenths are bigger than hundredths or thousandths" or "the more digits the smaller the number."

Adapted from M.E. Magone, J. Cai, E.A. Silver, and N. Wang, "Validating the Cognitive Complexity and Content Quality of a Mathematics Performance Assessment." *International Journal of Education Research* 21 (3) (1994): 317-340.

Figure 4.3 **An annotated reading assessment task of the type that might be used in NAEP reporting**

An interesting example of a forward-looking reading assessment comes from Michigan's recently implemented High School Proficiency Test. The basic structure of this exam involves students in reading and responding to three thematically related texts over two 50-minute periods. Initially, they encounter each passage independently, answering a few fairly traditional multiple-choice questions for each. Then, they answer some not so traditional multiple-choice questions that require them to integrate information and understandings across the passages, as shown in example X. The three passages accompanying these examples were, in turn, *The Loudest Cheer,* an article describing the obstacles that Curtis Pride, a deaf major league baseball player, had to overcome; *The Words of Chief Joseph,* a memoir of Chief Joseph of the Nez Perce Native American tribe; and *Heroes,* an account of four female heroes.

> ***Example X:***
> *Although they lived at different times and faced different problems, which word best describes Chief Joseph, Curt Pride, and the female heroes?*
> *a. athletic*
> *b. obedient*
> *c. weak*
> *d. determined*

When they return on day two, students are provided with this scenario for writing an essay in response to the three passages.

> ***Scenario:*** *Providing assistance (painting, shoveling snow, etc.) to senior citizens has been a community-service activity for members of the graduating class at the local high school for several years. On one of the work teams is a 12th-grade student who is new to the school district. The new student thinks that although the project is good, it needs to be reorganized.*

Figure 4.3 (cont)

Members of the team are having difficulty with the new student's suggestions on changing how the team works together. The team's methods have been successful for a long time. As a result, they do not give any major tasks to the new student.

Question: *Should the other members of the work team be more receptive to the new member's ideas? Why?*

Use your ideas, experiences, and knowledge, as well as the ideas in all of the reading selections, to write a thoughtful response to the question. Try to convince the reader of your position. Remember that you must use information and/or examples from all of the reading selections, as well as the titles of all the selections, to support your statements. You may make notes, list ideas, or otherwise plan your response before you begin writing.

Note the emphasis placed on using the knowledge gleaned from the three readings to construct a solution to this new problem, a definite emphasis on the application of knowledge gained from reading. This twin emphasis on knowledge and application is reflected in the scoring guide for this task, as evidenced in this description of the characteristics of a level 4 (the highest level obtainable) response.

Level 4
Knowledge: *The student's response demonstrates a synthesis of relevant knowledge with and across all three reading selections. It reveals depth and insightful connections without misconceptions about the reading selections, the scenario, and/or the scenario question.*

Figure 4.3 (cont)

Application: The student responds to the scenario question, stating a clear position which is supported effectively by examples from within all three and across at least two of the reading selections.

Specifically, the student must

▓ support the stated position with referenced examples from each reading selection.

▓ present a clear and thoughtful application of the common ideas, principles, and generalizations that connect all the reading selections.

To illustrate how this approach works, an exemplar response of a student paper, along with annotations depicting the way in which the response reflects the desired characteristics described in the rubric, is provided in example Y.

Figure 4.3 (cont)

Summary of comments from the Secondary Content Literacy Committee review of student responses:

This paper is a very good example of a student response to the questions asked related to the scenario. The author of this paper starts off with a clear position that is supported by references to the ideas in all three reading selections. Specific references, article titles, and quotes are used to effectively support the position.

Coming into a new situation or having a new person come into one's present situation are awkward ordeals, each of with take great care from both sides to be handled properly. Being unreceptive or descriminative to new or different people or ideas is a common mistake, and a shameful one.

A concise statement of the nub of the problem.

Curtis Pride's minor-league teammates obviously overlooked this point, when they mocked his physical handicap. But, as he shrewdly pointed out, "My handicap is deafness. Yours is intolerance. I'd rather have mine."

The same idea can be seen in the situation with the new student involved in the senior citizen service activity. The other twelfth-graders won't accept the new student, because they don't feel he/she is one of them.

A direct analogy made between the Curtis Pride situation and the senior citizen scenario; shows the use of evidence from text to support the thesis.

But much can be said for at least attempting to help. As seen in the "Heroes" section, any attempt to help, no matter how feeble it may seen, could prove to be very important. Trying to help should be appreciated for what it is: reaching out. No matter whether the idea will be used or not, all points of view should be considered. Besides, as Judy Jonas said, "Helping others is a moral obligation."

Another text-based example used to elaborate the thesis of tolerance of those who volunteer to help.

Figure 4.3 (cont)

First attempts will not alway get results. So it must also be realized that persistance in what one believes can make ever the deaf to hear (literally, in the case of Curtis Pride, when, despite his 95% hearing-loss, he heard the victorious crowd cheering for his magnificent hit). As he pointed out, "What matters isn't what they think, but what you think about yourself." Belief can work wonders.

But, as in the case of Chief Joseph, even persistance won't make everything better. Despite their efforts, the intolerance and closed minds of the white leaders at that time made them lose their home, as well as many loved ones. And Chief Joseph asked for acceptance, in the same way that the newcomer to the service activity should, "I only ask of the government to be treated as all other men are treated."

The author shifts audiences here and speaks to the "new student" offering encouragement for patience and persistence.

Here the author qualifies the persistence argument and returns to the basic thesis that tolerance and equity are the keys to effective community effort.

Overall:
Lots of evidence of knowledge of the themes of the three selections. No evidence of misconceptions. Repeated examples of applying story ideas to the scenario.

SOURCE: Michigan High School Proficiency Test

HIGH-VISIBILITY REPORTING

Relevant, engaging, and understandable achievement results increase the probability that these results will be understood and used. Yet, unless they are placed in high-visibility contexts such as widely read newspapers and popular non-print media, they cannot become part of the public debate on education and education reform. A number of creative possibilities for ensuring an adequate level of visibility exist. Advance arrangements could be negotiated with newspapers or magazines, for example, so that feature articles could appear at the time of new data releases, incorporating NAEP findings with commentary from influential thinkers and perhaps interest pieces about specific schools and students. Publications as diverse as the *New Yorker* or *Parade* magazine might be recruited into this effort to ensure that broad segments of the American public are reached.

Even greater visibility could be achieved through television news specials in which engaging and informative displays of what students can and cannot do are interspersed with commentary from members of Congress, education policy-makers, teachers, and parents. Another venue might be the establishment of a bi-annual White House Conference on the education achievement of the nation's school children that uses NAEP as the cornerstone for its message.

Other opportunities for expanding current conceptions of reporting include investing in the development of supportive materials (e.g., videos, training materials) that would allow users to more readily incorporate NAEP results into deliberations or conferences tailored to specific audiences. These audiences could be as diverse as professional groups of science educators, or the teachers or parent groups in a particular school or district. The October 2, 1996 *Education Week,* for example, carried a report of town meetings sponsored by two nonprofit organizations in order to stimulate engagement with education reform. In the meeting covered by the article, nearly 100 members of a suburban community came together to discuss such issues as vouchers and whether high schools should prepare students for jobs or college, or both.[2]   It is easy to imagine how such a debate could be informed by the kind of rich achievement data that helped to clarify the competencies required for work and higher education, and profiled the areas in which students were or were not achieving.

Finally, NAEP reporting must be predicated on the understanding that, in the coming decades, plain paper reports may be of value only as reference documents, if at all. NAEP already is making its various reports available through the World Wide Web, and the increasing ubiquitousness of Web access suggests that Web-based reporting should be expanded. Furthermore, reports should be adapted to take advantage of the Web's interactive and multimedia features. Besides offering "on-demand" availability, Web-based reports offer the potential for many other desirable features. They can include non-print materials such as video clips, can allow users much greater flexibility with regard to the level of detail at which they choose to engage the data, can provide automatic links to related information and help screens, and even can allow such interactive experiences as engagement with embedded assessments that can be completed and scored on-line.

The implementation of these ideas will require that the Department of Education and NCES play a more active role in making NAEP results more visible and informative. The Department will need to seek out appropriate forums for encouraging the debate NAEP results can help to inform. The Department also must help engage the public in these events by providing compelling examples along with NAEP results (including videotape of students problem-solving), and by being available to help interpret and debate their meaning.

FOSTERING CORRECT INTERPRETATIONS OF STATISTICAL FINDINGS

While portraying the scope and substance of student achievement at a given moment is one aspect of NAEP's mission, NAEP also is called upon to convey various trends and comparisons that require a certain level of statistical sophistication to present accurately. For example, because NAEP estimates are based on samples of students and samples of items, each estimate is associated with a certain amount of uncertainty related to the fact that some other sample from the same population could have yielded slightly different results. The measure of this uncertainty, commonly referred to as a standard error, is critically important for understanding such findings as the significance (or nonsignificance) of apparent differences between states. However, research on recent NAEP reports has shown that even groups of relatively sophisticated users have extremely limited understandings of these aspects of the data, and news reports of state NAEP results have erred repeatedly by presenting simple rank orderings of state scores without specifying which between-state differences are or are not significant.[3] Moreover, even the use of cumulative percentages in reporting results by achievement level has proved confusing to readers who expect percentages to add to 100 percent.[4]

These problems are not inconsequential, particularly when one considers the stated desires of the governors to use NAEP data to help monitor the outcomes of elementary and secondary education in their states. To understand the role of standard error in these judgments, consider the public/nonpublic school comparisons that were reported at the state level for the first time in 1994. As we pointed out with concern in our report on the evaluation of the 1994 TSA, the nature of the nonpublic school samples resulted in achievement estimates in which the confidence intervals[5] were very wide, certainly much wider than the corresponding confidence intervals for public school achievement. In Iowa, for example, the true average reading achievement score for fourth-grade public school students was almost certainly somewhere between 220.4 and 225.6 on the NAEP scale (a range of 5.2 points); for nonpublic school students, the corresponding score was estimated as being anywhere between 223.6 and 240.4 (a range of 16.8 points). However, the point estimates that were reported widely for the two types of Iowa schools were 223 for public and 232 for nonpublic. Reporting the results in this manner suggested a more reliable difference than actually could be demonstrated by the data.[6] In fact, the average reading achievement of all public school fourth graders in Iowa could have exceeded the average for all fourth graders in Iowa's nonpublic schools.

Resolving these communication difficulties is challenging, and NCES and others continue to investigate possible solutions. This effort must be given even greater attention in the coming decades if NAEP is to fulfill its promise for informing the public debate on education.

USE OF STANDARDS-BASED REPORTING

Finally, we turn to an aspect of reporting that spans both of the previous discussions because it is involved intimately with defining and describing achievement, but also partakes of problems of statistical inference and correct interpretation of numeric findings. This is the subject of standards-based reporting, currently embodied in the performance standards established by the Governing Board.

Standards-based reporting, or reporting in terms of what students *should* know and be able to do, is a departure from NAEP's original purpose, which was simply to describe what students know or *are* able to do. Yet the current education reform movement calls for reporting against standards, and the use of performance standards for NAEP responds to that call.

Nonetheless, our extensive evaluation of these achievement levels, conducted in 1992, raised serious questions about their reliability and validity, and subsequent work by NAGB has not mitigated our concerns. In particular, we believed that the level-setting process was unduly sensitive to surface characteristics of the items, such as whether they were multiple choice or constructed response, and that, consequently, the levels (operationalized as cutscores on the NAEP scale) would be unstable over time if the mix of item types changed in the assessment. Furthermore, based on comparisons with the distributions suggested by various non-NAEP measures, we concluded that the distributions of student performance established by the cutscores were not reasonable. In particular, the weight of the evidence suggested that the reading and mathematics cutscores were set too high, and did not correspond to the achievement-level descriptions as intended. Relatedly, we concluded that the prose descriptions and exemplar items that were chosen to represent the achievement levels did not represent accurately the student performances associated with score ranges delimited by the cutscores. A follow-up examination of the reading achievement levels in 1994 did little to reassure us that the problems identified in our evaluation of the 1992 achievement levels had been corrected.

What are the practical implications of such problems with the achievement levels? First, the potential instability of the levels may interfere with the accurate portrayal of trends. Second, the perception that few American students are attaining the high standards we have set for them may deflect attention to the wrong aspects of education reform. The public has indicated its interest in bench marking against international standards, yet it is noteworthy that, when American students performed very well on a 1991 international reading assessment,[7] these results were discounted because they were contradicted by poor performance against the—possibly flawed—NAEP reading achievement levels in the following year. Fruitful reform of American education must depend, not upon either scare tactics or white washing, but upon honest appraisal of the achievement of U.S. students, combined with a rich and accurate understanding of the nature of the achievement toward which we aspire.

In consequence, we repeat once again our earlier recommendation *that the current achievement levels be abandoned by the end of the century and replaced by new standards that reflect the multifaceted nature of achievement, and have been shown to be both reliable and valid.*

SUMMARY

NAEP reporting presents excellent opportunities for informing the American public about the kinds of achievement required for the 21st century and of the progress of our students in core subject areas. However, successful reporting also presents a number of challenges.

First, results must be presented as more than simple summary scores if they are to convey the richness of achievement. We suggest the use of score profiles that separately delineate various dimensions of achievement, as well as subscores for specialty areas within content domains.

Second, rich examples of student work should be used to engage the reader and explicate the more abstract scale scores and descriptions. At the same time, more aggressively creative reporting strategies should be pursued to ensure that the results are brought to the public notice, as well as being made conveniently accessible to educators and other decision-makers.

Third, research-and-development must continue in order to improve the communication of the statistical constructs that underlie correct interpretation of NAEP results.

Indeed, it is probably the case that successful reporting, in all of its aspects, is as challenging a problem as is adequate measurement of achievement. Both must be attended to if NAEP is to fulfill its mission as the nation's report card. *We therefore recommend that NAEP undertake a sustained and systematic research-and-development effort to improve the communication of assessment results.* The research program should include investigation of the costs and effectiveness of alternative formats for displaying and describing NAEP results as these affect audience interest, breadth of exposure, ability to understand results, and accuracy of interpretation. As part of this research venture, NAEP should explore the application of theories of adult learning to strategies for preparing NAEP audiences to understand and interpret NAEP correctly.

NOTES

[1] R. Forsyth, R.K. Hambleton, R.L. Linn, R. Mislevy, and W. Yen, *Design/Feasibility Team: Report to the National Governing Board.* July 1, 1996.

[2] A. Bradley, "Project Seeks Meeting of the Minds on Reform." *Education Week* (October 2, 1996).

[3] R.K. Hambleton and S.C. Slater, "Are NAEP Executive Summary Reports Understandable to Policy Makers and Educators?" Paper presented at the 1996 annual meeting of the National Council on Measurement in Education, New York, and R.M. Jaeger, "General Issues in Reporting of NAEP Trial State Assessment Results," in *Studies for the Evaluation of the National Assessment of Educational Progress (NAEP) Trial State Assessment* (Stanford, CA: The National Academy of Education, 1992).

[4] See R.K. Hambleton and S.C. Slater, ibid.

[5] The confidence interval is computed from the standard error and is the score range in which the state's true average achievement score almost certainly was located.

[6] The National Academy of Education 1996, op. cit., 43.

[7] Results from the International Education Association's International Reading Literacy Study. See W.B. Ellen, *How in the World Do Students Read?: IEA Study of Reading Literacy* (Hamburg: The International Association for the Evaluation of Educational Achievement, 1992).

CHAPTER 5:
CONNECTING TO THE
LARGER NETWORK OF EDUCATION
INFORMATION

IN THE EARLIER CHAPTERS OF THIS REPORT, we have argued for the central importance of utilizing NAEP's considerable resources to build and refine state-of-the-art measures of student achievement. Such measures should describe accurately what our students know and can do, cover the knowledge and skill base in core subject areas, and be based on dimensions of competency that are relevant to the needs of the 21st century. To maximize the utility of such a carefully crafted assessment system however, NAEP also must be well articulated with the larger network of education information required by an informed citizenry.

One way to accomplish this is to link NAEP to other assessments that provide achievement estimates for other populations of students so that comparisons across groups become possible. This would apply, for example, to linkages downward through state NAEP to the states' own assessments on the one hand, or upward to international assessments on the other. A second way in which to extend NAEP's value is to connect NAEP's achievement results, or use NAEP-developed assessment instruments in conjunction with studies that focus on education constructs such as school organization, instruction practices, and so on.

Linking to State Assessments

Current concepts of education reform have stressed the importance of providing feedback on student performance using assessments aligned with local curricula and standards. The best state and local assessments adhere to these principles, and increasing numbers of states are generating assessments that do so. However, because each state's assessment is tailored to its particular curricula and needs, states must look elsewhere for a more general measure of achievement that can provide a more universal basis for comparison. Moreover, the states are cognizant of the value of using external bench marks to validate their state assessment results and lend credibility to locally developed standards.

Since its inception in 1990, state NAEP has been providing this kind of external check for states who choose to participate, and we believe that it is important that any redesign be sensitive to the need for states to continue to use NAEP in this way. This would imply, for example, that NAEP should include grade levels and subject areas that are of interest to the states, and that NAEP maintain a predictable schedule of assessments around which states can plan.

Some states would like to be able to go further in this direction by statistically linking their state assessment results to those of NAEP. Linkages to states' own assessments are supported by the Governing Board in its principles for NAEP's redesign, and urged strongly by CCSSOs. Such linkages actually have been tried by a few states on an experimental basis. If shown to be technically defensible, such linkages would permit states to expand in several ways on the kinds of comparisons now possible through state participation in NAEP.

Of particular interest, sound linkages would allow states to express results on their state assessments for districts, schools, or individual students in terms of the NAEP scales and standards. They also would allow states to obtain such estimates for years in between state administrations of NAEP in a given subject area. It must be emphasized, however, that the "if shown to be technically defensible" is a non-trivial qualifier. *Although the statistical computations used for linkage can be applied to any pair of assessments, the linked results may lead to invalid inferences about student achievement if fairly stringent conditions for trustworthy linking are not met.* Moreover, a linkage between a state test and NAEP that is defensible at the time it is made may erode over time if, for example, the state test is susceptible to teaching to the test. That is, test specific preparation for the state test might improve scores on that test without producing generalizable increases in the underlying knowledge and skills measured by NAEP, thereby invalidating an earlier linkage.

Therefore, in determining when and how to undertake such linkages, certain technical points must be borne in mind. The first consideration is the comparability of the two assessments in terms of their content frameworks, overall design, assessment tasks, and conditions of administration. If, for example, one of the assessments covers a broader content domain, emphasizes different aspects of the curriculum, or is more or less reliable (consistent) in its measurement of achievement, then the linkage would be weaker and the resulting comparisons less stable and robust.[1] It is only now that research has begun to be done on the robustness of these various assumptions.

A solution for some of these problems might be possible if NCES and NAGB were to sustain NAEP as a fully comprehensive assessment—something for which we have argued throughout this report—but also were to generate separable modules within NAEP on which standards could be set for different aspects of achievement or different subcomponents of content. Under these conditions, states might be more likely to find a technically acceptable match to some subset of NAEP modules and thus effect a linkage to standards in at least part of the broad NAEP domain.

A related idea, being considered in the redesign and endorsed by the business leaders and governors at the 1996 education summit, is the possibility that some version of state NAEP could be administered as part of a state's assessment. An embedded state NAEP assessment might become more practical, for example, if shorter, booklet-length versions could be constructed to represent adequately key components of the achievement domain.

Such booklets could not, of course, be as comprehensive as the full NAEP. Work is needed to determine whether they could nevertheless capture, to a useful extent, the richer and more complex definitions of achievement that we encourage to be central to NAEP's primary mission. Furthermore, there is a separate reason for caution, in that embedding NAEP in this manner might make the assessment more high stakes and encourage "teaching to the test" in the narrow sense that erodes the generalizability of the results. If this were to happen, NAEP would lose much of its value as an external indicator and become simply one more test. *Finally, unless the sampling design and the conditions under which the assessment is administered remain the same, comparing the results from it with NAEP results is hazardous.*

The technical complexities of linking state tests to NAEP in ways that yield dependable results that support the desired generalization are thus formidable, but they are not necessarily insurmountable. School authorities are under increasing pressures to reduce testing burdens on students and classrooms from school, district, state, national, and international assessments. Local willingness to administer NAEP could wane and thereby undermine participation rates unless there are ways to link NAEP and state tests. Because the potential utility to states of linking state testing and NAEP is great, the goal is worth pursuing.

LINKING TO INTERNATIONAL ASSESSMENTS

While state and local assessments are particularly important, as these are the levels at which education decisions are made most frequently, there also is a demand to include international assessments in the network of education information. As we have noted earlier in the report, we live in an increasingly mobile society and global economy. Parents and policy-makers want to know how their students compare with other nations, as well as with other students within the United States. Using the same types of linking methodologies discussed above, it is hoped that NAEP can provide a bridge to international comparisons such as TIMSS—and via state NAEP—to state-to-international comparisons.

The pressure to make these linkages is increased by the expectation that U.S. education, its standards and assessments, is internationally competitive. The recent extensive media coverage of the IEA TIMSS study and intention to connect TIMSS and state NAEP results illustrates the intense public interest in creating these linkages.

Of course, the same cautions with regard to the comparability of the assessments and the robustness and stability of the linkage, noted under the discussion of state assessment links, also apply. Moreover, there are additional cautions regarding the interpretation of international comparisons because of the cross-national differences in curriculum, scope and sequence of instruction, distribution of opportunities to learn, instruction methods, rewards for superior performance, language, and cultural attitudes toward education.

INTEGRATION WITH OTHER SOURCES OF INFORMATION ABOUT AMERICAN EDUCATION

In order to provide a more complete context for understanding student achievement (and thereby enable achievement results to be used in a more policy-relevant manner), it would be extremely useful to integrate NAEP results with data on education inputs and school practice. Our vision is a data set that contains important variables at the student, classroom, school, district, and state level. Such a data set would provide a very fertile basis for hypothesis generation and the preliminary exploration of ideas about what matters in American education.

To bring this vision into reality, NCES should start now to explore the feasibility of integrating NAEP data with data from surveys that cover other aspects of the conditions of education. These include the Common Core of Data (CCD) and the Schools and Staffing Survey (SASS). The CCD is a comprehensive data base of all American schools that contains information on a fundamental, if somewhat limited, set of school variables, including enrollment size and type of school. The SASS, by contrast, surveys samples of U.S. schools to collect extensive data on a wide range of school resources and practices, including fiscal and administrative arrangements, teacher pay, and teacher preparation.

One of the technical problems that would have to be overcome in order to create such an integrated data base would involve determining how to align the separate samples. This is not a problem for CCD because that survey already includes all schools. In nearly every other case however, samples are used for efficiency. At the present time, for example, SASS samples in a way that produces inferences at the school level, whereas NAEP is designed to produce inferences about students. One could, nevertheless, generate overlapping subsamples that would allow accurate estimation of both sets of variables for the same schools.

NAEP AS A RESOURCE FOR OTHER DATA COLLECTION SYSTEMS

NCES also supports other data collection efforts, such as longitudinal studies of schools or students, that gather measures of both system inputs and student outputs. The National Education Longitudinal Study (NELS) is a prominent example. The challenge for these surveys is to maintain state-of-the-art measurement for the wide range of information they collect. Synergies and savings therefore could be affected if high-quality, modularized measures of each construct could be developed, then drawn upon by various studies for their purposes. NAEP is the obvious choice in which to invest in order to create premiere measures of student achievement. Indeed, NAEP assessments are already significantly more advanced than the achievement measures used by most other studies. NELS is a prime example; the short measures of verbal and mathematics ability it has used are far less adequate than NAEP-based measures would be—even if the latter were to be based solely on released booklets from NAEP's current assessments.[2]

Efficiency in the preparation of surveys and studies is not, however, the only reason for advocating such integration of measures. Secondary analyses become much more feasible when comparable measures have been used in various contexts. If different measures are used each time, the problems become very much like the problems associated with linking to state assessments. Each study will have measured something similar, yet not the same, and conclusions across studies will be more tenuous. The solution, therefore, is to overlap at least survey instruments—with each study incorporating at least some items from the other—even if the separate goals of the two studies preclude complete integration of measures.

The benefits of shared instruments and analyses become particularly salient when the two surveys cover different but related populations, or answer different but related questions. Thus, for example, it would be extremely interesting to compare, on the same scale, the achievements of 12th-grade students surveyed by NAEP with the achievements of young adults surveyed by the National Adult Literacy Survey (NALS). Similarly, overlapping NAEP and NELS measures would be helpful because NAEP provides information about the distribution of achievement in the whole population, while the longitudinal design of NELS provides better answers about how the achievement of particular individuals changes over time, as well as about school and non-school factors that may be influencing achievement.

SUMMARY

The value of NAEP will be enhanced considerably to the extent that it can be integrated with other sources of education information. If constructed in a technically defensible manner, links between NAEP and various state and international assessments would be particularly useful because they would allow different populations of students to be compared against a common set of scales and standards. In addition, interesting and insightful hypotheses concerning the relationship of student achievement to various conditions of education are likely if NAEP results can be combined with results from other NCES surveys such as CCD and SASS. Finally, NAEP can serve as a source of premiere measures of student achievement, to be drawn from by other studies that include student outputs among their concerns.

We recommend that NCES and NAGB immediately begin to further these goals. Appropriate use of linking can be facilitated, for example, by

■ *Making explicit the content and characteristics of the NAEP assessments;*

■ *Developing guidelines for appropriate linking applications using NAEP; and*

■ *Continuing research into linking methods and the validity of comparisons based on such links.*

NCES also should begin immediately to investigate ways of modifying sampling and data collection procedures so that school and staffing data gathered through SASS can be inferred to the same population as NAEP achievement data, and it can commit to using NAEP instrumentation, in whole or in part, in the next iterations of major surveys such as NALS or NELS.

NOTES

[1] For further discussion of these points, see R.L. Linn and V.L. Kiplinger, "Linking Statewide Tests to the National Assessment of Educational Progress: Stability of Results." *Applied Measurement in Education* 8 (1995): 135-155, and L. Bond and R.M. Jaeger, "The Judged Congruence Between Various State Assessment Tests in Mathematics and the 1990 National Assessment of Educational Progress Item Pool for Grade-8 Mathematics," in *The Trial State Assessment: Prospects and Realities: Background Studies* (Stanford, CA: The National Academy of Education, 1993).

[2] Of course, it would be necessary to maintain the security of nonreleased NAEP items and to protect NAEP from accountability-related uses that could encourage teaching to the test to ensure that the main purposes of NAEP would not be jeopardized.

CHAPTER 6:
PLANNING FOR THE LONG TERM

RECAPITULATION

NAEP PROVIDES RELIABLE AND ACCURATE DATA about student achievement, and, because it has shown its utility for states as well as for the nation, the demands for its use have grown dramatically. Much of this growth has occurred in less than a decade, and growth is likely to continue in coming years. Some advocate the use of NAEP for purposes of school-level accountability, and others would like to use NAEP as an individual student examination system. We believe these are not appropriate uses of NAEP. Instead, *we recommend that NAEP be used to provide periodic, up-to-date, state-of-the-art student achievement trend results that inform the ongoing debate about what American students know and/or should know for the 21st century.*

We have suggested that NAEP should be providing this information by 2015, but several changes are needed if this goal is to be met. *Of prime importance is our recommendation that NAEP adopt a substantially broader definition of achievement than is being* used currently, indicating that definition to the nation, and why the change is being made. In particular, NAEP must signal to schools, parents, and policy-makers that current definitions of achievement will not be sufficient to meet the demands of 21st century society. One way to do this is to provide richer information and examples about the competencies of the nation's children and adolescents. Therefore, *wherever the results support doing so, we recommend that NAEP content be reported using profiles of achievement (with separate subscores for knowledge and skills, problem solution and interpretation, and performance in groups), assuming that these profile scores can be shown to be valid and reliable.* In addition, NAEP should continue to report overall scores and content subscales where appropriate. Trends should be established to track improvement on each of these measures.

Second, NAEP should stimulate the debate about changes needed in American education by presenting the results in ways that capture the attention of parents, superintendents, teachers, and policy-makers at the national, state, and local level. Shortly after the results are released to the nation and the states, a series of informational events should be orchestrated. *We recommend that the Secretary of Education and Commissioner of Education Statistics encourage the major television networks, leading national newspapers, and other publications to do extended feature stories on what the nation's children know and don't know, accompanying descriptions of what they need to know.* This activity should be encouraged by making representatives of the Department available to work with the media on these projects, and by providing videotapes showing individual students and groups of students involved in the solution of challenging problems. *We also recommend that the Department make broadly available stimulating materials, including videotapes of actual student performance, that can be used to encourage discussions at the state and local level. The idea is to create an ongoing dialogue on education reform, encouraged and supported by the Department, using NAEP data and exemplar exercises. We further recommend a higher rate of task development in order to have a sufficient number of exemplary*

NAEP tasks available to share with the public. Research also is needed to ensure that these new approaches to reporting have the intended impact of encouraging meaningful discussions.

Third, we reiterate our concern that NAEP is being reported with a set of flawed performance standards (formerly called "achievement levels"). Given the growing importance and popularity of performance standards in reporting assessment results, it is important that the standards be set in defensible ways. Therefore, *we recommend the Governing Board and NCES undertake a thorough examination of the current performance standards, taking into consideration the relationship between the purposes for which standards are being set, and the conceptualization and implementation of the assessment itself. In addition, any new standards need to be shown to be reliable and valid for the purposes for which they are being set.*

Fourth, NCES has the opportunity to make NAEP more useful by both linking it with, and embedding it in, other relevant data sets. For example, if NAEP can be linked with state assessments in technically defensible ways, NAEP can be used as a way to check the validity of achievement trends in the states. Furthermore, if the link is sufficiently sound, state assessments could be used by schools and districts to link with national and international assessment results. Before such linkages are accepted and used for reporting state results however, it is critical that the links be shown to support the validity of the intended uses and interpretations. *The potential benefits to schools, districts, states, and the nation of being able to link NAEP to other assessments and data sets is great. We therefore recommend that research and trial tests be done on developing standards and guidelines for linking NAEP data to other assessments, including the validity of comparisons based on such links.*

Fifth, NCES has data sets, such as SASS and CCD, that could be used to investigate and generate hypotheses relating NAEP achievement to financial data, data on student-teacher ratios, and the like. Although studies using these data cannot be used to draw causal inferences, they could suggest hypotheses to be confirmed in other appropriately designed research studies. Another possibility is to embed blocks of NAEP tasks into other assessments (e.g., longitudinal studies such as NELS) as a way to facilitate comparisons between NAEP results and other assessments. While these possibilities are intriguing, *before embedding NAEP task blocks into other assessments or data sets, we recommend the development of standards and guidelines for doing so. Furthermore, research will be needed to assess the validity of results based on these uses of NAEP task blocks.*

Finally, we have given examples of how technology, either currently available or likely to be widely available in the next 10 to 15 years, may be used to create NAEP exercises that will allow the measurement of higher-order thinking processes in ways not currently available, and at relatively low costs. The realization of these potentialities will require investment in a sustained research-and-development program.

RECOMMENDATIONS FOR RESEARCH

In this report, we have made several suggested changes for NAEP in the year 2015. Planning a program of innovation of the kind suggested requires research, and we have summarized the most critical research needs below.

RESEARCH ON ASSESSING ACHIEVEMENT

The most important recommendation made in the report is that NAEP employ a broader definition of achievement, one that places great emphasis on understanding and the active use of knowledge. Between now and the year 2015, considerable research needs to be done to support this change. Although cognitive science has taught us a great deal in recent decades, its application to education is still in the relatively early stages. Therefore, we make the following recommendations for research:

■ *Additional basic research on the problem-solving model itself is needed. Although the problem-solving model appears to be useful for subjects such as science and mathematics, more research is needed even in these areas. Furthermore, even less is known about its applicability for other subjects such as reading, writing, history, the social sciences, and the arts. Based on what we have learned thus far however, we feel strongly that a significant investment in the application of cognitive science to classroom learning (and therefore to achievement and the assessment of achievement) is important, and we strongly recommend that it be made.*

■ *We have suggested the importance of a set of dimensions or components that describe problem solution, including knowledge and skills, problem representation, rules and strategies, metacognition, explanation, and interpretation. Basic research is recommended to determine the generality of these aspects and the extent to which specialization by subject matter is required.*

■ *The cognitive process model is dynamic and exhibits feedback between its various dimensions. The psychometric applications implied by this model are likely to be considerably different than the IRT model currently used with NAEP. Therefore, even while the cognitive process model is being refined, we recommend that research begin on psychometric applications implied by it.*

■ *Working in groups is an essential skill in contemporary society, and is likely to grow to be even more significant in the next century. Yet our understanding of group problem-solving is far from complete, and more needs to be known about how to assess individual contributions to group problem-solving. Therefore, we recommend that research on both group dynamics and individuals' contributions to group problem-solving be supported. Finally, the classroom provides a social context for learning. We need to know more about how that context affects learning and achievement. Therefore, we recommend that research on the role performed by social context in learning and achievement also be supported.*

▨ *Although there is a general concern about the use of multiple-choice items for the measurement of problem-solving, one should not simply assume that multiple-choice items are inappropriate and performance tasks preferable for assessing **all** aspects of achievement. Research has shown that it is relatively easy to build highly reliable scores using multiple-choice items, much more difficult with performance tasks, and that some dimensions of problem-solving clearly can be measured adequately with multiple-choice items. Others, however, cannot. Therefore, it is important to continue to refine and improve performance tasks. Research should be carried out on the generalizability of performance tasks under varying conditions of assessment. Research also is needed on the impact of guides used to score performance tasks; these can be an important source of variation when evaluating construct validity.*

RESEARCH ON THE USE OF TECHNOLOGY IN ASSESSMENT

In chapter 3, we argue for the importance of technology, especially computers, for NAEP assessment in the year 2015. Although the utility of technology already is being realized in many applications to assessment, much more research needs to be done to achieve the potential implied in this report and to ensure that such applications are not made prematurely.

- *Research should be undertaken in the use of computers to administer or score NAEP assessments. Of particular interest are adaptive testing applications that can make NAEP more comprehensive and cost-effective, as well as applications that would explicate the strategies and self-regulatory skills used to solve complex problems.*

- *Computers are being used already in group problem-solving and collaborative group-learning situations. We recommend that further research into these uses continue, including research on isolating and measuring individual contributions to group problem-solving.*

- *Finally, we recommend research on videotaping as a way of better understanding how students (including groups of students) solve problems. In addition, we recommend research on the use of video as an aid to scoring.*

RESEARCH ON THE ASSESSMENT OF SPECIAL NEEDS CHILDREN

The growing ethical and legal concerns about excluding special needs children from NAEP requires that more research be done on how to include more of them in NAEP by the year 2015.

- *We recommend that research continue to be done on accommodations and adaptations that might be made to the NAEP assessment that will allow meaningful participation for children with disabilities. Part of this effort should include research on the use of assistive devices to allow for participation of those with physical disabilities. This program of research also should address the issue of the construct validity of the accommodated assessments and demonstrate the range of accommodations over which comparisons with the standard NAEP assessment are warranted.*

▨ We also recommend continuing research on solutions to the problem of valid assessment of students for whom English is a second language. This should include the use of NAEP in languages other than English, as well as adaptations or accommodations that decrease the non-essential language requirements of the assessment exercises. The research must encompass both the increases in participation that can be achieved through such strategies and the construct validity of the resultant scores.

▨ Finally, cultural diversity continues to grow within the United States. The lenses through which children see and the ways in which they experience their neighborhoods, classrooms, and, indeed, the world more generally are shaped heavily by their cultural background. It is impossible to design a large-scale assessment that is sensitive to all of the issues associated with this diversity, but, when designing assessment tasks, for example, NAEP should take care to assess what children know and can do in ways that do not work to the detriment of those from different cultural backgrounds.

RESEARCH ON MOTIVATION

The validity of NAEP results for informing the nation presupposes that students participating in NAEP take the assessment seriously and try to do their best in responding to the exercises. However, there is a definite, if unproven, perception that group scores, at least for older students, are depressed by widespread problems of motivation.

▨ We recommend further research into the impact of student motivation on NAEP scores, in addition to research efforts aimed at creating assessment conditions that enhance student motivation.

Research on Reporting

Finally, NAEP must attend directly to the issues associated with successful reporting of NAEP. Several kinds of research are needed:

▨ *Before reporting NAEP results using profile scores (where the components would be knowledge and skills, problem solution and interpretation, and performance in groups), we recommend that research be done to demonstrate that such scores can be built in construct valid and reliable ways.*

▨ *We also recommend that NAEP undertake a sustained and systematic research-and-development effort to investigate the cost and effectiveness of alternative formats for displaying and describing NAEP results as these affect audience interest, breadth of exposure, ability to understand results, and accuracy of interpretation.*

The Need to Plan

The activities envisioned above will require substantial thinking through in addition to research and planning. If the planning process does not begin prior to the reauthorization of NAEP in 1998, it is unlikely that the proposed changes will occur, or, if they do, that they will be as cost-effective as they could have been. For this reason, *we endorse the Peat Marwick recommendation that NAGB and NCES immediately begin to undertake strategic planning for NAEP.* As their report emphasizes, good planning is an ongoing exercise, not an activity that occurs once a year or once a decade. As was well done in the development of the NAGB redesign document, it is important to involve key stakeholders in the planning process. Although not all planning depends upon funding for NAEP, much of it does. *We therefore also recommend that Congress help underwrite planfulness by guaranteeing funding for NAEP at least four to five years in advance.* Without such guarantees, much of the planning needed to effect the suggestions made in this report will be impossible.

What are some of the areas that require better planning?

First, *if states are going to be able to take full advantage of NAEP in their programmatic efforts and assessment programs, they need a known assessment schedule with subject areas, grades to be assessed, and years of assessment essentially guaranteed.*

Second, *better planning is required to protect core NAEP operations from disruptions caused by the introduction of unplanned changes in NAEP operations and methods—disruptions that can affect the overall quality of NAEP.* We agree with NAGB's Design Feasibility Team that no change in the design of NAEP should be introduced that has not been thoroughly field-tested as part of an overall assessment plan.[1] Major changes, such as many of those envisioned in this report, likely will require several iterations that are evaluated in an ongoing research-and-development program prior to large-scale field-testing and eventual incorporation into operational assessments. Quick-fix, last-minute design and procedural changes can become costly errors and also are liable to lead to problems with comparability of results across assessments.

Third, *better planning and accompanying research studies, as indicated above, are needed to allow for the iterative development of new methods, procedures, and items.* We agree with the Design Feasibility Team that no changes in design, methods, or procedures should be made without first trying to ensure that they are not creating unanticipated and negative effects for the assessment. The best example of how such tinkering can affect assessment results is the 1986 NAEP reading anomaly.

Fourth, *framework development should be a process that begins up to five years in advance of the implementation of an assessment.* A framework must be agreed upon by diverse stakeholders. Because the stakeholders often represent divergent points of view about what should be taught and assessed in a given content area, it can be very difficult and time-consuming to achieve consensus. Procedures need to be developed for representing the convergences and divergences of various perspectives, and generating a statement of current and future knowledge, and skill requirements. Developing the framework also includes designing the task specifications. As mentioned in chapter 3, some of the past performance tasks have been scored in ways that are not true to the purpose for which the task was written. This problem can be reduced through carefully written task specifications and empirical try-out of item types before the specifications are finalized. *We recommend that at least 18 months should be available for the development of task specifications for each subject-matter area assessed by NAEP.*

Fifth, *because the enriched conceptualization of achievement suggested in this report requires the use of many performance tasks, far more time also is going to be needed to write, review, and field-test tasks for future NAEP assessments.* Good performance tasks take significantly longer to write than good multiple-choice or short-answer items. After the questions are written, a careful review needs to be done that includes a review of the scoring guides and that ensures that there are sufficient items to measure the various facets of achievement. Research that combines cognitive and psychometric analyses is required to develop strong methods for establishing the construct validity of performance items in assessing the various dimensions of achievement. Finally, the items need to be field-tested, a procedure that takes several months to complete. The items need to be analyzed to make certain they are working as designed. Those that are not working appropriately need to be revised and further field-tested.

To ensure that all these steps occur in a coordinated and timely manner will require substantial planning on the part of the Governing Board and NCES. Furthermore, the entire process should involve advice and review of subject-matter specialists. NCES has established standing committees of subject-matter specialists to participate in this process. We commend NCES for following this recommendation. However, *because we believe the activities of the subject-matter panels are so important, we recommend that the Commissioner appoint their members. Doing so will raise the visibility, legitimacy, and influence of the panels.*

Sixth, NCES and NAGB need to plan for the introduction of new trend lines at the same time that new frameworks are introduced. Building on the position taken in chapter 3, *we recommend that, when a new trend line is introduced, the old trend line be continued for at least one more 8- through 10-year cycle. Ideally, we would like to see trend lines run, on average, for 20 years before ending them. As the current NAEP long-term trend results demonstrate, it can take four or five assessment cycles to verify whether changes in a trend line are real or aberrant.*

We further recommend that NAGB and NCES develop a long-range plan for overlapping trend lines. Such a plan requires the commitment to parallel activities that span the time interval of the individual trend lines (e.g., framework revision, item development, item tryouts, etc.), including trying out any changes in methods or procedures that could introduce assessment error prior to introducing them into the assessment. We recommend that these parallel activities begin roughly five years before the introduction of a new content-area framework.

COMING FULL CIRCLE

We end this report by reminding the reader of how we began. As the nation debates the quality of our education system, it is imperative that we have trustworthy data on whether our students are learning what they need to know to be productive and informed citizens in the 21st century. While we have suggested several ways in which NAEP can be even more useful in the first decades of the 21st century than it has in its nearly

30-year life, we continue to believe strongly that its fundamental purpose is to inform the public and policy-makers about student achievement in the states and in the nation. We have suggested that, in order that our students meet the broad challenges of the 21st century, a new, broader definition of achievement will be needed.

Students must leave schools with a well-developed, integrated knowledge base that can be used to engage in effective problem-solving, including the ability to draw correct inferences, make defensible interpretations, and challenge questionable assertions. In order to be able to provide valid information about students' progress in meeting these achievement goals, NAEP also must employ a broader definition of achievement than it has in the past.

When providing information to the public about how well our students are achieving in school, NAEP should simultaneously stimulate democratic discussion and debate about how to better improve the education our children receive. If NAEP can play the role of reporting valid and trustworthy data in a way that will stimulate such debate, it will have played a critically important role in the improvement of American education as we move into the 21st century.

NOTES

1 R. Forsyth, R.K. Hambleton, R.L. Linn, R. Mislevy, and W. Yen, op. cit.

APPENDIX
GUIDING PRINCIPLES

NAEP's MISSION AS AN INDEPENDENT INDICATOR OF STUDENT ACHIEVEMENT

The National Indicator Principle

NAEP should continue to be the key independent indicator of what the nation's students know and can do, providing trend data on student academic performance in key subject areas.

The State Indicator Principle

Because states have constitutional authority for education, NAEP should continue to play an additional, needed role by proving independent information to the states on the educational progress of their students.

The International Indicator Principle

The United States must compare its education practices and results with those of other nations and, where possible, learn from the education practices of others. NAEP should therefore, to the extent possible, be linked with major international assessments.

NAEP's Fundamental Criteria of Excellence: Quality and Utility

The Quality Principle

NAEP should be exemplary in the development and use of assessment and reporting techniques and practices that produce reliable, fair, and valid estimates of student achievement.

The Utility Principle

The NAEP data and program must be useful for a variety of stakeholders, including policy-makers, the public, educators, and researchers.

Principles for Enabling NAEP Excellence

The Comprehensiveness Principle

NAEP frameworks and content must be comprehensive, reflecting both the range of current education practice, sound theory, and research about human learning and performance.

The Relative Stability Principle

NAEP frameworks must be in place long enough and assessed regularly enough to establish meaningful trend lines. At the same time, the framework revision process must remain attuned to the natural evolution that occurs in subject-matter fields.

The Inclusiveness Principle

To the degree technically, ethically, and financially possible, NAEP should assess an inclusive sample of all children in the designated age or grade populations.

The Policy Relevance Principle

NAEP must collect data relevant for policy-makers and education decision-makers, and report the data in a timely fashion, while maintaining its integrity uncorrupted by political pressures.

The Public Information Principle

NAEP data and reports must be accurate in content, comprehensive in format, and readily accessible to all relevant stakeholders.

ASSESSMENT IN TRANSITION: MONITORING THE NATION'S EDUCATIONAL PROGRESS

CODA

FROM 1989 TO 1996, this Panel brought together a set of dedicated and thoughtful individuals to conduct an independent evaluation of the National Assessment of Educational Progress (NAEP) Trial State Assessments (TSAs). Our members, appointed by The National Academy of Education (NAE), took their work seriously, generating five reports over a six-and-one-half-year period.

We commissioned numerous papers and studies to provide ideas for our debate and data for our various reports. In the course of this work, we identified important issues and contributed to solutions that we believe will enhance NAEP's future. Throughout, we benefited from the strength of our members—people who speak well about what they know—schools, subject matter, psychometrics, and how children learn.

The following list includes all members since the Panel's inception.

CHAIRS

Robert Glaser
Learning Research and Development Center,
University of Pittsburgh
1989-1996

Robert L. Linn
University of Colorado at Boulder
1989-1996

MEMBERS

Anthony Alvarado
New York City Board
of Education
1994-1996

Gordon M. Ambach
Council of Chief State
School Officers
1989-1996

Isabel Beck
University of Pittsburgh
1989-1993

Lloyd Bond
University of North Carolina at
Greensboro
1989-1996

Ann Brown
University of California
at Berkeley
1989-1996

Robert M. Groves
University of Michigan
1989-1996

Edward Haertel
Stanford University
1992-1994

Richard M. Jaeger
University of North Carolina at
Greensboro
1994-1996

Lyle V. Jones
University of North Carolina at
Chapel Hill
1989-1996

Mary M. Lindquist
Columbus State University
1994-1996

Iris Carl
National Council of Teachers of Mathematics
1989-1993

David K. Cohen
Michigan State University
1989-1992

Ramon Cortines
Formerly, San Francisco School District
1989-1992

Alonzo Crim
Georgia State University and Spelman College
1989-1996

Linda Darling Hammond
Columbia University
1989-1992

Pasquale J. DeVito
Rhode Island Department of Education
1994-1996

Edmund W. Gordon
Yale University and City University of New York
1994-1996

P. David Pearson
Michigan State University
1994-1996

Edward Roeber
Council of Chief State School Officers
1989-1996

Albert Shanker
American Federation of Teachers
1989-1996

Lorrie M. Shepard
University of Colorado at Boulder
1989-1996

Marshall Smith
Formerly, Stanford University
1989-1993

William Winter
Former Governor, State of Mississippi
1989-1992

Lauress Wise
Human Resources Research Organization
1994-1996

Project Director
George W. Bohrnstedt
American Institutes for Research
1989-1996

Associate Project Director
Frances Stancavage
American Institutes for Research
1990-1996

RESEARCH CONTRIBUTORS AND COMMISSIONED INVESTIGATORS

The Panel expresses its gratitude to the distinguished researchers who carried out the commissioned investigations that formed the backbone of our evaluation. This stellar group, through papers and studies, provided insight and invaluable advice in their areas of expertise. Some contributors later joined us as members of the Panel.

The Panel extends thanks to P. David Pearson of Michigan State University and Lizanne DeStefano of the University of Illinois at Urbana-Champaign for their contributions to the content validation of the 1992 and 1994 reading assessments, and the evaluation of the 1992 reading achievement levels. Thanks also to Peter Afflerbach of the University of Maryland for his work with David and Lizanne on the 1994 reading assessment content validation, and to Diane Bottomley, Cheryl Ann Bullock, Matthew Hanson, and Cindi Rucinski of the University of Illinois and Urbana-Champaign, who joined David and Lizanne to investigate the relationship between achievement levels and teachers' and researchers' ratings of student performance. The Panel also acknowledges Bertram C. Bruce and Jean Osborn of the University of Illinois at Urbana-Champaign and Michelle Commeyras of the University of Georgia for their early work on the content and curricular validity of the 1992 reading framework. For their analysis of the 1994 drop in reading scores, the Panel thanks Larry Hedges of the University of Chicago and Richard Venezky of the University of Delaware.

Thanks to Edward Silver, Patricia Ann Kenney, and Leslie Salmon-Cox of the Learning Research and Development Center at the University of Pittsburgh for their content validation of the 1990 mathematics assessment, and to Ed and Pat for their further work on the validation of the 1992 assessment and their expert review of the 1992 mathematics achievement levels. For their work evaluating the 1992 writing achievement levels, the Panel thanks John Hayes of Carnegie Mellon University and Glynda Hull of the University of California at Berkeley.

For his extensive work on issues of sampling and survey design, which informed four of our five reports to Congress, the Panel thanks Bruce Spencer of Northwestern University. The Panel also thanks Albert Beaton and Eugenio Gonzalez of Boston College for their study concerning international comparisons with NAEP results. For their assistance on issues of reporting NAEP results below the state level, the Panel thanks Ramsay Selden of the Council of Chief State School Officers (now executive director of the Education Statistical Services Institute [ESSI]), and Walter Haney and George Madaus of Boston College. The Panel also offers appreciation to Richard Jaeger of the University of North Carolina at Greensboro for his exploration of general issues in reporting the NAEP TSA and for his work, with Lloyd Bond, to investigate the congruence between various state assessment tests in mathematics and the 1990 NAEP mathematics assessment. Edward Haertel of Stanford University gave the Panel the benefits of his insights into the extent of reasonable inferences that can be made from TSA results.

Specific to this capstone report, the Panel thanks Eva Baker of the University of California at Los Angeles for her writings on the potential of technological applications for NAEP, and James Greeno of the Institute for Research on Learning of Stanford University, P. David Pearson of Michigan State University, and Alan Schoenfeld of the University of California for their work on the implications of learning and cognition research. The Panel also thanks Darrell Bock of the University of Chicago for his proposals for the design of a modified NAEP scaling methodology, Richard Elmore of Harvard University for his work on adjusted scores, and Jack Jennings and Diane Stark of the Center on National Education Policy for policy issues related to the use of NAEP and NAEP scores. For a consideration of issues surrounding science performance assessments, the Panel thanks Richard Shavelson of Stanford University, and for their paper on the participation of students with limited English proficiency, Kenji Hakuta and Guadalupe Valdés of Stanford University.

The Panel is appreciative of the work of James Yesseldyke, Kevin McGrew, and Martha Thurlow of the National Center for Educational Outcomes, who provided consultation for the Panel's study of assessability and exclusions of students with disabilities, and of Walter Secada of the University of Wisconsin for his work on issues in the development of a Spanish language NAEP.

Some individuals made particular contributions in the form of studies and papers while serving on the Panel. These include Robert Linn and Lorrie Shepard, who, in collaboration with Elizabeth Hartka of the American Institutes for Research (AIR), investigated the influence of choice of content, statistics, and subpopulation breakdowns on the relative standing of states in the 1990 TSA, Edward Roeber, who collaborated with Frances Stancavage and George Bohrnstedt on studies of the impact and reporting of the 1990 TSA, and Lyle Jones and Pasquale DeVito, each of whom wrote papers addressing perspectives on the future of NAEP for this capstone report. A special thanks as well to Lorrie Shepard for her central role in authoring the Panel's second report to Congress: *Setting Performance Standards for Student Achievement.*

The Panel is particularly thankful to the many staff from AIR who carried out studies and papers; they include the following.

For studies of the administration and costs of the TSAs, Donald McLaughlin, Elizabeth Hartka, Frances Stancavage, Catherine Godlewski, Jay Chambers, Jin-Ying Yu, Kadriye Erickan, and Dey Ehrlich. For a study of the impact of public school nonparticipation, Elizabeth Hartka, Marianne Perie, and Donald McLaughlin. For a substantial body of studies on the validity of the 1992 achievement levels, Donald McLaughlin. For studies relating to the exclusion and assessability of students with disabilities or limited English proficiency, Frances Stancavage, Donald McLaughlin, Elizabeth Hartka, Robert Vergun, Catherine Godlewski, and Jill Allen. For a survey of expert opinion on the content validity of the 1992 reading framework, Julia Mitchell, and for work on the validity of the achievement levels used to report the 1992 and 1994 reading results, George Bohrnstedt and Evelyn Hawkins. For studies on the impact and reporting of the 1992 and 1994 TSAs, Frances Stancavage, Evelyn Hawkins, and Elizabeth Hartka. Finally, for their collaboration on the above mentioned investigation of the relationship between achievement levels and teachers' and researchers' ratings of student performance, Donald McLaughlin, Phyllis DuBois, Marian Eaton, Frances Stancavage, Catherine O'Donnell, and Jin-Ying Yu.

Thanks also to report writers, editors, and all-important administrative staff who have kept this project functioning. At AIR these include, in addition to George Bohrnstedt and Frances Stancavage, Donald McLaughlin, Elizabeth Hartka, Phyllis DuBois, Jennifer O'Day, John Olson, Michelle Bullwinkle, Lorna Bennie, Elise McCandless, Shannon Daugherty, Jean Wolman, Audrey Struve, and Josephine Morrisey, as well as Jeremy Finn (State University of New York, Buffalo), who made significant contributions to the Panel's third report during one summer at AIR. At the University of Pittsburgh we thank Elizabeth Rangel, Cindy Yockel, and Michelle von Koch. At The National Academy of Education our thanks go to Debbie Leong-Childs and her associate Sunny Toy. The Panel also wishes to acknowledge the special contributions of Bella Rosenberg of the American Federation of Teaching, particularly for her thoughtful reviews of each of the Panel reports.

Finally, the Panel thanks all the students, teachers, administrators at state departments of education, state assessment directors and curriculum specialists, and other policy-makers and educators who responded to various surveys, provided data, and helped carry out information searches involved in the production of the various reports.

NATIONAL CENTER FOR EDUCATION STATISTICS

The Panel acknowledges the indispensable support provided by staff at the National Center for Education Statistics (NCES). Information, practical assistance, and reasoned advice all have been available throughout the course of the evaluations, greatly facilitating our work. In particular, retired Commissioner Emerson Elliott and his immediate successor, Acting Commissioner Jeanne Griffith, provided thoughtful guidance at many project junctions, and current Commissioner Pascal Forgione has continued to do so. The Panel especially acknowledges the support of Associate Commissioner Gary Phillips, Sharif Shakrani, Larry Ogle, and Steve Gorman, each of whom have played very active roles in securing required technical materials and keeping the Panel apprised of NCES' plans and activities. Tongsoo Song helped oversee the administration of the grant and fulfill its contractual details in the early days. Also early in the Panel's work, Eugene Owen was central to facilitating a productive and harmonious working relationship between NCES and the Panel. The responsiveness and helpfulness of these NCES staff greatly assisted the Panel's investigations and kept the project moving on a fast track.

CONTRACTORS

Without the courteous and professional collaboration of the NAEP contractors, the Panel's evaluations could not have been completed in a timely fashion. Among the many Educational Testing Service (ETS) staff who contributed to our work were Eugene Johnson, who provided extensive information and advice concerning NAEP's psychometric procedures, John Mazzeo, who played a key role on a wide range of topics, Jay Campbell, who answered many questions about the reading assessment and also coordinated the special scoring for the

Panel's accessability studies, Dave Freund and Patricia O'Reilly, who oversaw the preparation of data sets, and Debbie Kline, who coordinated responses to technical questions on the 1994 assessment. Other ETS staff who provided ongoing long-term support for multiple studies include Jules Goodison, John Olson (now at ESSI), Kent Ashworth, Claudia Gentile, Bruce Kaplan, Steve Koffler, Steve Lazar, Don Rock, and Al Rogers, as well as Barry Druesne of the College Board and Walter MacDonald of Advanced Placement. Of special help was Ina Mullis, longtime project director for NAEP and now at Boston College.

Staff at Westat gave considerable advice and assistance concerning NAEP's sampling, administration, and data processing procedures. Special thanks are due Nancy Caldwell and Diane Walsh for facilitating the recruitment of schools, Keith Rust, who supplied vast amounts of materials and information, Chris Schroeder, who played an important role in arranging observations of classroom administrations for the first TSA, and Annelle Bond, Lesly Flemming, Brice Hart, Cindy Randall, and Sandy Rieder. At National Computer Systems (NCS), Brad Thayer expedited the flow of administration documents and Lynn Zaback provided Panel staff with important data.

OTHER ORGANIZATIONS AND GOVERNMENTAL AGENCIES

The Panel also extends thanks to the many staff at American College Testing (ACT) who graciously provided data and welcomed Panel observers to meetings of the achievement-level setting panels, the revisit of the reading achievement levels, and the Technical Advisory Committee for Standard Setting. Mel Webb and Susan Loomis, in particular, provided technical support and information, as did Howard Garrison of Aspen Systems. Special thanks also are due to the National Assessment Governing Board (NAGB) staff, including Roy Truby, Mary Lyn

Bourque, Mary Crovo, Ray Fields, Dan Taylor, and Larry Feinberg for their cooperation and prompt response to requests for information. At the Council of Chief State School Officers (CCSSO), Ramsay Selden, Rolf Blank, and Barbara Kapinus all joined with Panel members Gordon Ambach and Ed Roeber to assist in obtaining necessary information and keeping up to date with state affairs. Kevin Crowe and, later, Cadelle Hemphill were especially helpful in coordinating with the assessment subcommittee of CCSSO's Educational Information Advisory Committee, which also welcomed us to its meetings and deliberations.

The Panel sincerely appreciates the academic and government specialists who spoke at Panel meetings, providing information that ranged from historic perspectives to leading research on NAEP and the TSA. For this role, the Panel thanks Terry Hartle, Andrew Hartman, Jack Jennings, Chauncey Jones, and Renee Slobaski.

For all of the above, we have been extremely fortunate in our collaboration, and we hope the best for the future work of those connected with informing the nation about its education health.

The Capstone Report

The Panel members who are particularly responsible for the capstone report include

Chairs

Robert Glaser
*Learning Research and Development Center,
University of Pittsburgh*

Robert L. Linn
University of Colorado at Boulder

Gordon M. Ambach
*Council of Chief State
School Officers*

Mary M. Lindquist
Columbus State University

Lloyd Bond
*University of North Carolina
at Greensboro*

P. David Pearson
Michigan State University

Alonzo Crim
*Georgia State University and
Spelman College*

Edward Roeber
*Council of Chief State
School Officers*

Pasquale J. DeVito
*Rhode Island Department of
Education*

Albert Shanker
American Federation of Teachers

Edmund W. Gordon
*Yale University and City
University of New York*

Lorrie M. Shepard
University of Colorado at Boulder

Richard M. Jaeger
*University of North Carolina at
Greensboro*

Lauress Wise
*Human Resources Research
Organization*

Lyle V. Jones
University of North Carolina at Chapel Hill

Project Director

George W. Bohrnstedt

American Institutes for Research

Associate Project Director

Frances Stancavage

American Institutes for Research

THE PANEL'S OTHER REPORTS

Assessing Student Achievement in the States
The First Report of The National Academy of Education Panel
on the Evaluation of the NAEP Trial State Assessment: 1990
Trial State Assessment (1992)

Setting Performance Standards for Student Achievement
A Report of The National Academy of Education Panel on the
Evaluation of the NAEP Trial State Assessment: An Evaluation
of the 1992 Achievement Levels (1993)

The Trial State Assessment: Prospects and Realities
The Third Report of The National Academy of Education Panel
on the Evaluation of the NAEP Trial State Assessment: 1992
Trial Sate Assessment (1993)

*Quality and Utility: The 1994 Trial State Assessment
in Reading*
The Fourth Report of The National Academy of Education Panel
on the Evaluation of the NAEP Trial State Assessment: 1994
Trial State Assessment in Reading (1996)

REFERENCES

Alexander, L., and James, H.T. *The Nation's Report Card: Improving the Assessment of Student Achievement.* Washington, DC: The National Academy of Education, 1987.

Baker, E.L. "Learning-Based Assessment of History Understanding." Educational Psychologist 29 (2) (1994): 97-106.

Baker, E.L. "Readying the National Assessment of Educational Progress to Meet the Future," in *Assessment in Transition: Monitoring the Nation's Educational Progress, Background Studies.* Stanford, CA: The National Academy of Education, 1997.

Baxter, G., and Glaser, R. *Cognitive Analysis of Science Performance Assessments.* Los Angeles, CA: UCLA Graduate School of Education, Center for Research, Standards, and Student Testing, forthcoming.

Beck, I.L., McKeown, M.G., Worthy, J., Sandora, C.A., and Kucan, L. "Questioning the Author: A Year-Long Classroom Implementation to Engage Students with Text." The Elementary School Journal 96 (4) (1996): 387-416.

Bond, L., and Jaeger, R.M. "The Judged Congruence Between Various State Assessment Tests in Mathematics and the 1990 National Assessment of Educational Progress Item Pool for Grade-8 Mathematics," in *The Trial State Assessment: Prospects and Realities: Background Studies.* Stanford, CA: The National Academy of Education, 1993.

Bradley, A. "Project Seeks Meeting of the Minds on Reform."
Education Week (October 2, 1996).

Britt, M.A., Marron, M.A., and Perfetti, C.A. *Students'
Recognition and Recall of Argument Information in History Texts.
Annual Report for the National Research Center on Student
Learning.* Washington, DC: Office of Educational Research
and Improvement, U.S. Department of Education, 1994.

Brown, A.L., and Palinscar, A.S. "Guided, Cooperative Learning
and Individual Knowledge Acquisition," in L.B. Resnick, Ed.
*Knowing, Learning, and Instruction: Essays in Honor of Robert
Glaser.* Hillsdale, NJ: Lawrence Erlbaum Associates, 1989.

Brown, A.L., and Campione, J.C. "Guided Discovery in a
Community of Learners," in K. McGilly, Ed. *Classroom
Lessons: Integrating Cognitive Theory and Classroom Practice.*
Cambridge, MA: Bradford Books MIT Press, 1994.

Lawton, M. "Geography Courses Have Little Effect for Seniors,
Final NAEP Report Says." Education Week XV (40) (July 10,
1996): 5.

Ellen, W.B. *How in the World Do Students Read?: IEA Study of
Reading Literacy.* Hamburg: The International Association for
the Evaluation of Educational Achievement, 1992.

Flower, L., Hayes, J.R., Carey, L., Schriver, K., and Stratman, J.
"Detection, Diagnosis, and the Strategies of Revision." College
Composition and Communication 37 (1) (1986): 16-55.

Forsyth, R., Hambleton, R.K., Linn, R.L., Mislevy, R., and Yen,
W. *Design/Feasibility Team: Report to the National Governing
Board.* July 1, 1996.

Greeno, J.G., Pearson, P.D., and Schoenfeld, A.H. "Implications for the National Assessment of Educational Progress of Research on Learning and Cognition," in *Assessment in Transition: Monitoring the Nation's Educational Progress, Background Studies.* Stanford, CA: The National Academy of Education, 1997.

Hambleton, R.K., and Slater, S.C. "Are NAEP Executive Summary Reports Understandable to Policy Makers and Educators?" Paper presented at the 1996 annual meeting of the National Council on Measurement in Education, New York.

Jaeger, R.M. "General Issues in Reporting of NAEP Trial State Assessment Results," in *Studies for the Evaluation of the National Assessment of Educational Progress (NAEP) Trial State Assessment.* Stanford, CA: The National Academy of Education, 1992.

Jones, L.V. "A History of the National Assessment of Educational Progress and Some Questions About Its Future." Educational Measurement 25 (1996).

Jones, L.V. "The National Assessment of Educational Progress, Origins and Prospects," in *Assessment in Transition: Monitoring the Nation's Educational Progress, Background Studies.* Stanford, CA: The National Academy of Education, 1997.

Kiplinger, V.L., and Linn, R.L. *Raising the Stakes of Test Administration: The Impact of Student Performance on NAEP.* Los Angeles, CA: UCLA Center for the Study of Evaluation, 1992.

KPMG Peat Marwick and Mathtech. *A Review of the National Assessment of Educational Progress: Management and Methodological Procedures.* Washington, DC: 1996.

Lane, S. "The Conceptual Framework for the Development of a Mathematics Assessment Instrument." Educational Measurement: Issues and Practice 12 (2) (1993): 16-23.

Linn, R.L., and Kiplinger, V.L. "Linking Statewide Tests to the National Assessment of Educational Progress: Stability of Results." Applied Measurement in Education 8 (1995): 135-155.

Linn, R.L., Koretz, D., and Baker, E.L. "Assessing the Validity of the National Assessment of Educational Progress: Final Report of the NAEP Technical Review Panel." Report to the National Center for Education Statistics, 1995.

Magone, M.E., Cai, J., Silver, E.A., and Wang, N. "Validating the Cognitive Complexity and Content Quality of a Mathematics Performance Assessment." International Journal of Education Research 21 (3) (1994): 317-340.

The National Academy of Education. *Assessing Student Achievement in the States.* Stanford, CA: 1992.

The National Academy of Education. *Setting Performance Standards for Student Achievement.* Stanford, CA: 1992.

The National Academy of Education. *The Trial State Assessment: Prospects and Realities.* Stanford, CA: 1993.

The National Academy of Education. *Quality and Utility: The 1994 Trial State Assessment in Reading.* Stanford, CA: 1996.

National Assessment Governing Board. *Positions on the Future of National Assessment of Educational Progress, 1993.* Washington, DC: 1993.

National Assessment Governing Board. *Policy Statement on Redesigning the National Assessment of Educational Progress.* Washington, DC: August 2, 1996.

National Council of Teachers of Mathematics. *Curriculum and Evaluation Standards for School Mathematics.* Reston, VA: 1989.

National Education Summit Policy Statement. National Education Summit. March 26-27, 1996.

O'Neil, Jr., H.F., Sugrue, B., Abedi, J., Baker, E.L., and Golan, S. *Final Report of Experimental Studies on Motivation and NAEP Test Performance.* Los Angeles, CA: UCLA Center for the Study of Evaluation, 1992.

O'Neil, Jr., H.F., Sugrue, B., and Baker, E.L. "Effects of Motivational Interventions on NAEP Mathematics Performance." Educational Assessment (in press).

Public Law 103-227. Goals 2000: Educate America Act: March 1994.

Public Law 102-119. The Individuals with Disabilities Education Act: 1991.

Raghavan, K., Sartoris, M.L., and Glaser, R. "Interconnecting Science and Mathematics Concepts: Area and Volume," in R. Lehrer and D. Chazan, Eds. *Designing Learning Environments for Developing Understanding of Geometry and Space.* Mahwah, NJ: Erlbaum, in press.

Scardamalia, M., and Bereiter, C. "Higher Levels of Agency for Children in Knowledge Building: A Challenge for the Design of New Knowledge Media." The Journal of the Learning Sciences 1 (1991): 37-68.

Secretary's Commission on Achieving Necessary Skills, U.S. Department of Labor. *Skills and Tasks for Jobs: A SCANS Report for America 2000.* Washington, DC: U.S. Department of Labor, 1991.

Secretary's Commission on Achieving Necessary Skills, U.S. Department of Labor. *Learning a Living: A Blueprint for High Performance. A SCANS Report for America 2000.* Washington DC: U.S. Department of Labor, 1992.

Shanker, A. "How much do our kids really know?" The New York Times (July 29, 1990).

Shavelson, R.J. "On a Science Performance Assessment Technology: Implications for the Future of the National Assessment of Educational Progress," in *Assessment in Transition: Monitoring the Nation's Educational Progress, Background Studies.* Stanford, CA: The National Academy of Education, 1997.

Womer, F.B. *What is National Assessment?* Ann Arbor, MI: National Assessment of Educational Progress, 1970.